Modern innovations
in the teaching of reading
Donald and Louise M. Moyle

University of London Press Ltd
for the United Kingdom Reading Association

Acknowledgments

The authors and publishers would like to thank the following
for permission to reproduce material in the book:
Ward Lock Educational Ltd for the initial teaching alphabet
on page 24 taken from *The Teaching of Reading* by Donald
Moyle; John Murray and the i.t.a. Foundation for the
example of i.t.a. on page 24, John Murray and Professor Wijk
for the example of Wijk's 'Regularized Inglish' on page 25,
and John Murray and Professor Fry for the example of the
Diacritical Marking System on page 26—these three examples
are all taken from *i.t.a. An Independent Evaluation* by
F. W. Warburton and V. Southgate; and lastly *Special
Education* for the chart which appeared in Donald Moyle's
article for the June 1970 issue.

University of London Press Ltd
St Paul's House, Warwick Lane, London EC4P 4AH
Printed and bound in Britain by
Hazell Watson and Viney Ltd, Aylesbury, Bucks

Contents

Preface

So many books are being published in the education field today that it is very difficult for teachers to keep in touch with research and new developments. This series of monographs has been devised both to collate new ideas and to save teachers of reading from having to spend much of their valuable time searching out relevant texts and materials.

Each monograph will deal with a specific problem area (for example, modern innovations in teaching reading, reading readiness, the development of fluency, problems of assessment), giving a review of theoretical considerations and published research, and pointing out their important practical implications.

Professor J. E. Meritt
Department of Educational Studies
The Open University, Bletchley

Introduction

The popular as well as the educational press has regularly drawn attention in recent years to apparent deficiencies in the reading standards in this country. Complaints have ranged from the number of children who leave school without having reached a functional level of literacy, to the numerous undergraduates who have not sufficiently mastered the higher order reading skills necessary to undertake a degree course successfully.

It is not our purpose here to enter into a discussion of reading standards, but the concern expressed has had positive results, as shown by the many attempts to facilitate reading growth by the production of new materials, media and methods. Indeed, the past decade has seen more innovations than the previous fifty years produced. The primary purpose of this small volume will therefore be to describe the various approaches and materials which have appeared in recent years so that teachers may be helped to choose those most suited to their own teaching situation. Since each approach involves a particular view of the nature of the reading process, the rationale upon which each has been based will also be discussed.

In looking at these innovations we will examine the strengths and weaknesses of each in turn. Of course we have no intention of trying to seek out one method or set of materials which is superior to all others. Our knowledge of the learning process involved in reading is far from complete and research indicates that success is more relative to the teacher and child than to the methods or materials employed. The enthusiasm and expertise of the teacher will of course be more apparent when he or she is happy with the approach being used. Also, of course, children vary in the methods which are most suited to them as individuals and in the materials which they find stimulating and attractive. Though it will not be possible for class teachers to have in their possession the total range of equipment, an attempt will be made to suggest which materials and methods are most suited to children with certain needs.

There are many approaches to be considered. We have however attempted over the years to use these methods in the classroom in both normal and remedial situations. When this has not been possible the use of the materials by other teachers has been observed. However, the reader will appreciate that it has not been possible to follow the progress of children using the more recent innovations over long periods of time. Finally, brief comments will be made upon research that has tried to assess each approach and a list of books for further reading is supplied so that more detailed knowledge of each approach may be obtained.

Chapter 1 Whole-word Methods

This heading covers a variety of activities which will almost always be present to some degree in reading work but which form the major part of the approach to reading for some teachers. In many ways the language-experience approach would seem to be the most natural and realistic way of gaining development in reading, especially with young children. Basically it is a wide language-arts programme with an emphasis upon the relationship between reading and speaking, listening, writing and spelling. The raw material of the programme exists in the child's own experiences which he is encouraged to discuss. The aim is that the child will gradually come to appreciate the value of language. Next he learns that if he can say something, it can be represented in print. At first his ideas will be written by the teacher but later he can write them out himself. The child realises that when he has written something he can read it and soon will be able to read what others have written.

The language-experience approach is then a natural approach insofar as it is based on the logical development of language and on the necessity of the human race to communicate. Along with his own individual experience the child will have group experiences and here the importance of communication becomes even more obvious. Further, the teacher will be able to structure and develop growth in language and in reading by providing experiences which enrich and extend the child's knowledge of vocabulary. Children seem to progress quickly to the stage where they want to record their experiences in a more permanent form than speech and so pictures, captions, small books, newsheets, etc. begin to be produced.

Reading is of course a means to an end and not an end in itself so it is always important that, when the child reads or writes, the material used is sufficiently interesting and vital to be worth the effort. In some American schools this language-experience approach has developed into a sequence of arid experience charts where the children are given a set of pre-selected experiences. Under such a system all the major advantages in terms of motivation to use language tend to be lost.

The traditional approach to reading via the reading scheme is

11

often criticised because of the limited vocabulary which often makes the text stilted and almost meaningless to the children. Thus although the language-experience approach with a wide vocabulary has relevance at all stages of reading development, it has particular importance in the infant school. Used well it will result not only in good reading attainment but also in the establishment of good attitudes towards reading and learning generally.

In common with all other approaches there are both advantages and disadvantages in basing all reading-development lessons solely on language-experience work. Its advantages lie in its vital connection with the child's interests which should ensure adequate motivation, the use of the child's own language which ensures understanding and its informality which should minimise any sense of failure. The disadvantages are the difficulties of establishing a growth structure, of ensuring the development of the sub-skills and a core vocabulary which will enable the child to go to a book with success. Any teacher employing this method widely will need to have a very thorough knowledge of the growth structure involved in the reading process and also a detailed knowledge of each individual child.

It would seem, therefore, that for the greatest success, the marriage of this approach to some more structural type of learning, say a linguistic approach, could draw together the best of both worlds during the early stages of reading development.

When some facility in reading has been achieved the use of this approach can be widened considerably. A good deal of reading growth will be achieved almost incidentally as projects and centres of interest are undertaken. A useful means of extending this approach is provided by the Experience-Exchange Scheme which was a central theme at the 1970 Annual Study Congress of the United Kingdom Reading Association (UKRA). (Further information concerning this scheme can be obtained from Mr D. G. Mitchell whose address is included in Appendix 3.) Briefly, children exchange letters, results of surveys and projects. Among the advantages of such work are the realism it lends to the learning process, the added interest and thus motivation to the learning process generally. Lastly, but by no means least, it encourages a high standard of presentation and a critical attitude towards both personal work and the efforts of others.

Everyweek Educational Press

In recent years a number of reading schemes have appeared which make some use of language-experience approaches (for example, *Time for Reading*). It is sometimes difficult, however, to match particular centres of interest to a given stage of reading development.

The appearance of the Everyweek Educational Press publications have to some extent overcome this difficulty. There are now four weekly papers appearing ten times per term:

My News for children aged four to five
Our World for children aged six to seven
Read for children aged eight to nine
Everyweek for children aged ten to twelve.

These papers are not intended to be substitutes for a reading scheme nor in fact is their primary aim to teach reading. Rather they present material which is felt to be of interest to the children and which will motivate them to read and to explore their environment. A useful stimulus is provided by each child receiving his very own paper each week. Again they widen the area of interest of the child in a way that would be difficult for the individual teacher in the confines of a single classroom.

Each paper has its own weekly teachers' bulletin which gives further information and suggestions for work based upon the material presented in the children's paper. Also included are articles on topics of general educational interest or accounts of particular approaches or pieces of work.

A large number of schools now take one or more of these papers. Obviously they are used to greatest advantage when the stimulus supplied is used by the teacher to good effect. Perhaps the best use lies somewhere between the two extremes of just handing them out to the children and carrying our slavishly every suggestion offered by the authors.

Further reading
GODDARD, N. L. (revised edition 1969) *Reading in the Modern Infants' School*. London: University of London Press.
. Describes an approach to reading in the infant school based largely on language-experience approaches. Includes many suggestions for topics and apparatus.
VILSCEK, E. C. (1968) (ed.) 'Using Language Experiences in Beginning Reading.' In *A Decade of Innovations*. Newark, Delaware: International Reading Association (IRA).
A description of language-experience approaches in American

schools with a review of research findings and a discussion of the advantages and disadvantages of the method.

WHOLE-WORD APPROACHES

Over the past few years a controversy has raged concerning the respective merits of whole-word and phonic approaches to the teaching of reading, particularly in the early stages of learning to read. Research has shown that neither approach has any great advantage over the other and this is possibly due to the fact that both approaches cover a whole range of methods which tend to merge into one another. This is seen very clearly in the work of Gates who provided exercises with detailed letter discrimination in workbooks accompanying readers, which had a predominantly look-say approach: for example, 'underline the word which is the same as the first one

big // pig dig bag big gig'

Though this is intended to be a visual exercise it is almost identical to the type of work which accompanies many phonic schemes where perhaps the emphasis would be on 'sounding' the letters.

Schonell (1949)* was correct in suggesting that reading necessitates the ability to see words as units and also to see them as being composed of individual letters. However, there is no real evidence for the assertion that whole-word approaches should be used in the early stages and phonic approaches when some facility has been achieved.

Comenius suggested a whole-word or look-say approach to reading in the sixteenth century and many students trained in English training colleges prior to the 1914–18 war were advised of the method. However, though it was no doubt used by many teachers it was not nearly so widely used as were phonic methods until the late 1940s when teachers in infant schools felt that whole-word approaches were much more in keeping with the child-centred movement in education which was becoming increasingly influential.

Though teachers were often heard to suggest they used a look-say method it was perhaps more true to state that many were no longer teaching reading but rather immersing the child in a rich environment and expecting them to learn the skill for themselves. At this time there was an increase in the number and quality of books available for young children and teachers felt that they could now release their pupils from the tedium of sessions of phonic drill.

* All references are given on p. 95 ff.

14

Janet and John Reading Scheme

This scheme was first published in Britain in 1949, and the Teachers' Manual professes that it is a 'whole-word' approach. However there is also a parallel scheme referred to as a 'phonic' approach. The scheme had already been used extensively in other English-speaking countries. The popularity of the scheme can be seen from the fact that new books are still being added to the extension-reader part of the scheme. Indeed, Goodacre (1967) in a survey of the teaching of reading in 116 London schools found that this scheme was used as a basis for the teaching of reading in more than half of the schools. This popularity is not surprising when one realises that it provides an enormous number of books and equipment, rivalled only by *Happy Venture* (Schonell's 'mixed-methods' scheme). The expense of changing to a new scheme compared with renewing worn books from the existing scheme tends to inhibit change. Its introduction was well-timed for teachers were looking for more attractive illustrations and a release from phonic drills. They believed that vocabulary control offered security to the child whilst more up-to-date material would prevent the boredom and lack of reality at that time associated with phonic schemes.

The basic course consists of seven readers in the whole-word edition (or six readers if the phonic edition is chosen) and eight extension readers. There are also thirty-nine supplementary readers, workbooks, comprehension cards, word and sentence flashcards, a big book of pictures, word and picture matching cards, drawing books, jig-saw puzzles, stand-up figures and a picture dictionary. Rarely however does one find schools which have and use the full range of materials available—many teachers use supplementary activities of their own design at various points in the scheme.

The basis of the approach is that the child first associates pictures and words and then memorises them by regular controlled practice. Later on the new words introduced must be learned from the context or introduced from outside the scheme by the teacher. As the child must memorise the words, those used in the early part of the scheme are chosen to be as different in visual pattern as possible so that the child is not confused.

This, of course, limits the story content and often results in language which is very remote from that used in normal conversation by children. Thus the first two readers of the basic scheme are rather stilted and present a real problem to some children. The books quickly become very long and it is felt that Books 3 to 8 should be cut to approximately half their present length. At

15

their present length the young child feels that he is never going to manage to get to the end of such immense tomes. The illustrations, though no doubt much above average in 1949, now leave much to be desired. Often they do not clearly relate to the text and are, therefore, unhelpful. The phonic-approach books are almost the same as those of the whole-word approach. Only slight changes are made but special word lists are given at the back of each book. It is therefore necessary in both series that the teacher provide extra work in this area outside the scheme, assuming that it is accepted that some acquaintance with phonics is necessary to reading growth. Boys using this scheme seem to need this extra help more than girls in order to achieve success for it has been found that this series of readers tends to accentuate the well-known phenomenon that girls achieve fluency rather more speedily than boys. It may be, of course, that this is more closely related to the type of story material than the whole-word approach.

The aim of the scheme as expressed in the manual is 'that children should gain without drudgery or wasted effort a reliable foundation of reading knowledge on which further knowledge can be built'. Certainly many children have learned to read with this scheme without any extra work of the kind which was felt necessary by Gates. Experience seems to point, however, to the fact that the higher level of attainment is reached in infant classes using this scheme when the teacher does undertake additional work, particularly in writing and phonics, and when the child reads to the teacher with considerable frequency. In other words neither the scheme itself nor the approach employed has proved to be the hoped for cure-all for reading difficulties, but it has provided a step forward in the attempt to find more realistic and successful approaches to the teaching of reading.

Ladybird Key Words Reading Scheme

This scheme consists of thirty-six books, wall pictures, matching materials, drawing books, workbooks and flashcards. The *Greenwood Tapes* and cards for the *Language Master* (see page 70) have been produced to further extend the range of equipment available. The books are divided into twelve stages and within each stage there are two story books and an activities book which involves comprehension work and from the fourth stage some phonic work. The three books within each stage use identical vocabulary.

Though some phonic work is introduced the scheme uses basically a whole-word approach, and represents an advance on the majority of infant reading schemes in that the choice of words used is based on research. Before Murray wrote the scheme, he and McNally (1962) undertook an analysis of children's literature in order to find the most used words. They compared and amended their work in the light of other such studies and produced a list of 300 words which appeared to represent 75 per cent of words used in children's texts. Obviously if these words were mastered early the child could achieve independence and use the context efficiently at an earlier date. Stories written from these words would also seem more likely to reflect the experience and interests of children than those stories based on words chosen for the wide differences in their appearance.

The scheme has become popular in both infant schools and remedial work and this is no doubt due in part to the advance shown in its construction. It is also of course attractively produced and far cheaper than any comparable set of material. Mass production resulting in low cost is not of course without its disadvantages. Some children come to feel that the standard size and close similarity of the vast range of Ladybird books means that they are all very much the same inside, so there can be a loss of motivation. Again it is not always an advantage to have the books readily available for purchase by parents at every newsagent's shop.

In places the text is stilted and attractive pictures are linked to text which is lacking in meaning and interest value. As a scheme it emphasises teaching rather than learning and its full value will only be gained when the teacher is constantly involved. When this is so, meaning can be given to the sparse text of the early books in relation to the pictures presented.

Given these limitations the scheme is still proving very successful though from the middle of the scheme onwards the grading is rather steep for the slow learner. The work in the 'C' series, particularly that in phonics, could be greatly extended and the teacher will often find it necessary to devise supplementary work if maximum growth is to be obtained. Well used it can be of value as a central scheme in the infant or junior school.

Further reading
MCNALLY, J. and MURRAY, W. (1962) *Key Words to Literacy.* London: The Schoolmaster Publishing Co.
Lists the 'key' words, describes the research undertaken to draw up the list and suggests ways of teaching the words.
MURRAY, W. (1969) *Teaching Reading.* Loughborough: Wills and Hepworth.
The teachers' handbook to the *Key Words Reading Scheme*

which includes a simple description of the reading process and ideas for apparatus related to the scheme.

Racing to Read

In producing this series of sixteen readers based on the whole-word approach Tansley and Nicholls based their work on a rather different type of research. They took into consideration Burrough's (1957) analysis of children's conversational speech and also the free writing work of children. This would seem an even more realistic way than an analysis of the vocabulary of children's books for it is the language of the children which is being used and both vocabulary and sentence patterns are thus in keeping with those of the children.

This scheme made an outstanding contribution to reading growth among junior school children who had not made any progress in reading hitherto. Most teachers find however that the scheme needs some extra work in the form of workbooks or tapes for maximum efficiency. This series has recently been extended and revised to have a more attractive visual presentation. Tansley intends that from roughly the middle of this scheme children should also work from his phonic scheme *Sound Sense*.

Words Your Children Use

Edwards and Gibbon (1964) conducted a wide investigation into the vocabulary used by children in their written work and have produced lists of these words, arranged according to the frequency of usage by children in the 5-, 6- and 7-year-old age groups. For the teacher making reading materials and apparatus or for one using a language-experience approach, these lists form a very handy source.

Edwards and Gibbon have used this vocabulary as the basis of a series of interest and reference books for young children in their *Our World Series* (1966). These are well produced and they also provide a structure which can form a background to a language-experience approach.

Research and materials for whole-word approaches have to date placed the main emphasis upon vocabulary. This is of course only part of the reading process for often a child can recognise and understand all the words and still not understand the idea expressed in a sentence because the structure of the sentence is unfamiliar to him. It is hoped that publishers will pay more attention to both factors in the production of reading materials in the future.

18

Further reading
EDWARDS, R. P. A. and GIBBON, V. (1964) *Words Your Children Use.* London: Burke Publishing Co.
Contains the word lists with a description of the research on which they were based.

VISUAL-VERBAL APPROACH

We have examined some approaches in the realm of whole-word methods where an attempt has been made to select the words used in a scientific manner. The visual-verbal approach concentrates more upon the method of learning by a look-say approach and therefore has more to say about teaching procedures than choice of words. Indeed, in the early stages the vocabulary is largely selected on the basis of a language-experience approach in that the words used are suggested by the children.

The early stages of the look-say approach involve the association of word and picture but this approach often results in children guessing the word from the picture without ever looking at the word itself. Webster suggests therefore that the child should find it impossible to look at the picture without viewing the word and that the emphasis should gradually move from the picture to the word.

The process suggested is one which has links with conditioning. The basic unit of equipment is the visual-verbal card. This is simply a folded piece of paper. The top side bears the word and a bold picture is placed on the inside of the card so that when it is glued down the picture lies immediately behind the word but cannot be seen. The children play race games with these cards. They must first look at the word but if they cannot make an attempt they hold the card up to the light and the picture appears with the word still super-imposed upon it. Capital letters are used extensively at this stage for Webster feels that they are more likely to inculcate appreciation of the importance of letter sequence to the word than lower case letters which may well involve the child guessing the word from some 'sticking-out' feature. A whole series of materials and games are built on this foundation.

The visual-verbal approach is a mixture of look-say and language-experience though phonic work is built into the approach later. If the full range of materials is produced it can be an exciting and effective approach, particularly in remedial work. Teachers must be warned against picking out an odd game and welding it into their existing work for unrelated activities do not seem to have much long term value. At present the teacher must produce material for this approach as it has not been published but after the early work Webster's reading series *Rescue Reading* would fit in very well.

Further reading

WEBSTER, J. (1965) *Practical Reading*. London: Evans.
A description of the visual-verbal method and instructions for design of the apparatus.

Chapter 2 Medium Modification and Cueing Techniques

When the first steps in learning to read present difficulty and are dragged out over a long period of time the child is unlikely to develop those attitudes and enthusiasms which will give him an interest in reading as an activity. There is some evidence that one of the stumbling blocks to reading progress is the irregularity of the sound/symbol relationships of the English language. Some have felt that a modification of the reading medium would enable the child to master the early steps in reading more quickly and in recent years a good deal of experimentation and innovation has been focused upon this type of approach.

There are two major ways in which the printed medium can be changed in order to increase the sound/symbol relationship in the eyes of the child. The first is to change the spelling of English words so that they are more easily equated with speech sounds. The best known example of this type of modification is i.t.a. The second method is to use a signalling system which, whilst retaining the traditional spelling, will point the child to the sound which any letter or group of letters should make. In the eighteenth and nineteenth centuries a number of attempts to achieve this were made by using diacritical marking systems. Here the original words were accompanied by various dashes and squiggles which gave directions as to what sound was represented by the letters. In order to master reading by such a method the child must of course learn a second code as well as all the varied sounds with which letters can be associated. Although many teachers still use some sort of marking system in their classrooms, usually with vowel combinations only, few books have been published incorporating this technique. Some teachers have used Johnson's system which was devised as a spelling aid for helping children to read and this is incorporated in three books. In America Fry (1966) has been experimenting with his own system but results to date are not impressive.

A second and much more popular signalling system is the use of colour. Children are attracted by colour so there is a motivation factor as well as the regularising factor inherent in such material. The problem of the learning of a second coding system is still present of course. A range of uses have been made of colour but they fall into two major classes. Either all sounds can be given a colour and the letters representing this sound are

printed in the colour or the colour can point the child to a particular phonic rule. *Words in Colour* is an example of the former,
and *Reading by Rainbow* an example of the latter, whilst *Colour
Story Reading* employs both uses of colour in order to simplify
the medium.

MODIFIED ALPHABETS

Initial Teaching Alphabet

The Initial Teaching Alphabet has been the most publicised
innovation in reading in recent years but it must be remembered
that it is not a method of teaching reading, it is a simplification
of the material to be read. Indeed in the early days of research
into i.t.a. the teachers using the medium were requested to
employ the teaching methods they had used when teaching
reading through the medium of traditional orthography. Sir James
Pitman drew the origins of i.t.a. from 'Phonotopy' which was
designed by his grandfather and which was used briefly in a
modified form in both America and Britain in the 1850s. Sir
James produced his new alphabet which he called the Augmented
Roman Alphabet and it was launched as a research project in
1960 supervised by the Reading Research Unit of London
University, Institute of Education.

Pitman felt that the inability of some children to read and the
painfully slow progress of many other children were directly
related to the difficulties inherent in our language. The English
language is undoubtedly full of inconsistencies in its phoneme/
grapheme correspondence. Thus the same letter or group of
letters is pronounced differently in different words whilst the
same sound can often be spelt in a variety of ways. Hodges and
Rudorf (1965) after a massive computer study of English words
concluded that only 50 per cent can be spelled according to rules.
Pitman has estimated that only 40 per cent of English can be
strictly called regular, that is having perfect phoneme/grapheme
correspondence. Pitman aimed to provide a regularised medium
which children could use in the early stages of reading and his
alphabet is claimed to be in the region of 95 per cent consistent
in its sound symbol relationship.

A further reading difficulty can arise for some children from
the variety of type faces used in reading books. The peculiar
'a's' and 'g's' are not found quite so frequently nowadays but
some printers still use serifs whilst others do not, often making
it necessary for children to learn two representations of the same
letter. In i.t.a. the print is standard. Majuscules replace capital

letters and these are simply a larger version of the equivalent lower-case letter. There are forty-four characters in the i.t.a. though in its first form there were only forty-three. These are made up of twenty-four letters from the traditional alphabet and twenty new symbols many of which are designed to present a single representation in print of diphthongs or digraphs. The sound symbol relationship of English could be even more consistent but this would either greatly increase the number of symbols or reduce the visual relationship to traditional orthography. In either case transfer to traditional orthography at a later stage would be rendered more difficult.

Pitman's i.t.a. has not been the only attempt in recent years to produce an initial teaching medium. Indeed, consideration was given to Wijks' *Regularized English* before the Reading Research Unit chose i.t.a. for its experiment. In America the use of Unifon has been gaining ground of late. Wijk's suggested spelling system looks rather more like traditional orthography than i.t.a. in that only the existing twenty-six letters of our alphabet are employed. Unifon on the other hand is more difficult for the uninitiated to read than is i.t.a. but it has a more precise sound-symbol relationship.

In designing a simplified spelling system as an introduction to reading the problem is to strike a balance between regularity of sound-symbol relationship in order to gain a speedy start to reading for the child and to ease the transfer to traditional spelling when he has achieved fluency within the regularised medium.

Pitman claimed that children who start learning to read with his alphabet would learn to read more quickly, ultimately become more proficient, and be able to transfer to traditional orthography without difficulty. Two large researches took place between 1961 and 1967 under the direction of John Downing and many other smaller projects on both sides of the Atlantic have been reported. It is probably true to say that no other curriculum innovation has been subjected to such intensive testing as i.t.a.

Early evidence appeared fully to justify all the claims made by Pitman and also suggested some grounds for thinking that comprehension, spelling and free written work may ultimately be helped by the medium. However, later researches have not demonstrated such overall superiority for i.t.a. Warburton and Southgate (1969), reviewing the evidence published to early 1967, consider that though children using i.t.a. master reading more quickly in the early stages than do those working in traditional orthography (t.o.) there appear to be no significant differences between the two groups after three years when all children work in t.o. Longer follow-up of children needs to be undertaken for apple arm angel author bed cat chair doll eel egg finger girl hat

a   ɑ   æ   au   b   c   ɕh   ɖ   ɛɛ   e   f   g   h

tie ink jam kitten lion man nest king toe on book food out oil

ɪe   i   j   k   l   m   n   ŋ   œ   o   ω   ꙍ   ou   oi

pig red bird soap ship treasure tree three mother due up van window

p   r   ɼ   s   ʃh   ʒ   t   ʧh   ʧh   ue   u   v   w

wheel yellow zoo is

wh   y   z   ƨ

The initial teaching alphabet

tradiʃhonally wun ov ʃhe first tasks ov ʃhe infant scꙍl woƨ tω teeɕh ɕhildren tω reeɖ. it iƨ still, kwiet rietly, a mæjor pre-occuepæʃhon, sins reeɖiŋ iƨ a kɛɛ tω muɕh ov ʃhe lɛrniŋ ʃhat will cum læter anɖ tω ʃhe possibility ov independent study. in meny infant scꙍlƨ, reeɖiŋ anɖ rietiŋ ɑr treeteɖ aƨ ekstenʃhonƨ ov spœken laŋgwæj. ʃhœƨ ɕhildren hꙍ hav not haɖ ʃhe opportuenity at ·hœm tω grasp ʃhe pɑrt ʃhat ʃhæ plæ ɑr introɖuest tω ʃhem bie ʃhe everydæ events anɖ envieronment ov ʃhe classrꙍm. messæjeƨ tω gœ hœm, letterƨ tω sick ɕhildren, læbelƨ tω enʃhuer ʃhat matɛɛrialƨ anɖ tꙍlƨ ɑr returnɖ tω ʃhær proper plæs; aull caull for reeɖiŋ anɖ rietiŋ. meny ɕhildren first glimps ʃhe pleʒuerƨ ov reeɖiŋ from liseniŋ tω storiƨ reɖ tω ʃhem at scꙍl. . . . bꙍks mæd bie teeɕherƨ and ɕhildren about ʃhe ɖꙍiŋƨ ov ʃhe class or ov individuealƨ in it figuer prominently amuŋ ʃhe bꙍks whiɕh ɕhildren enjoi. ʃhæ help ɕhildren tω sɛɛ mɛɛniŋ in reeɖiŋ anɖ tω appreeʃhiæt ʃhe purpos ov ritten recordƨ.

A passage in i.t.a.

Traditionally one of the first tasks of the infant school was to teach children to read. It is still, quite rightly, a major preoccupation, since reading is a key to much of the learning that will come later and to the possibility of independent study. In many infant schools, reading and writing are treated as extensions of spoken language. Those children who have not had the opportunity at home to grasp the part that they play are introduced to them by the everyday events and environment of the classroom. Messages to go home, letters to sick children, labels to ensure that materials and tools are returned to their proper place; all call for reading and writing. Many children first glimpse the pleasures of reading from listening to stories read to them at school .... Books made by teachers and children about the doings of the class or of individuals in it figure prominently among

Fry's Diacritical Marking System

Traditionally wun ov the first taasks ov the infant scoole woz to teach children to read. It iz still, quite rightly, a major preoccupation, since reading iz a kee to much ov the lerning that will cum later and to the possibility ov independent studdy. In meny infant scooles, reading and writing ar treated az extensions ov spoken language. Thoze children hoo hav not had the opportunity at home to graasp the part that they play ar introduced to them by the everyday events and environment ov the claasroome. Messages to go home, letters to sick children, labels to enshure that materials and tooles ar returnd to their proper place; aul caul for reading and writing. Meny children first glimpse the plezures ov reading from lissening to stories red to them at scoole .... Books made by teachers and children about the dooings ov the claas or ov individuals in it figur prominently amung the books which children enjoy. They help children to see meaning in reading and to appreciate the purpos ov written records.

Wijk's Regularised Inglish

it to be ascertained that this quick commencement upon reading might result in better attitudes and an increased independence in language work which could influence progress significantly further on in school life. Almost ten per cent of primary schools in Britain and about the same percentage in North America are now making some use of i.t.a. Consequently there is now a fund of experience upon which teachers can draw when making a personal decision concerning the relevance of the approach to their own situation.

In the early days there was a great shortage of reading material but now over one hundred publishers have produced more than 1 000 titles in i.t.a. and in areas where schools are using i.t.a. the public library has usually a stock of books for out-of-school reading. There is no need therefore for children to be starved of reading material if they use i.t.a. but there are other limitations. They cannot directly relate the print from their normal environment, television viewing etc. to reading in school. Again many of the reading schemes available are existing reading schemes transliterated into i.t.a. whereas the medium itself would suggest a different type of reading scheme which at once could be more carefully structured and yet wider in vocabulary and type of reading material.

The regularity of i.t.a. at first sight invites a phonic approach and a number of teachers use a quite traditional approach to phonics and gain considerable success. The American *Early to Read* scheme, specially written for work in i.t.a., employs such a phonic approach and some research suggests that children learning i.t.a. with a phonic bias are more successful than those using a 'look-say' approach (Tudor-Hart, 1969). However, if the advantages offered by i.t.a. are improved attitudes towards reading, a speedy beginning to reading and the ability to write down one's own ideas and report experiences, the small advantage gained by using a phonic approach to word recognition would not seem to be of major importance. Best use is possibly made of i.t.a. when a programme based mainly on language-experience is offered, backed up by systematic help in the more mechanical aspects of reading when this seems necessary for the individual child.

It is possible, however, that transfer may be eased if some type of work leading to an understanding of the spelling patterns of English is undertaken gradually. Most teachers using i.t.a. suggest that transfer to traditional orthography does not present any problem once fluency is reached in i.t.a. Research suggests that some children at least have considerable problems in making the adjustment and most children receive a temporary setback

(Downing 1967). One reason for this could be that having worked in a largely regular medium for so long children find it harder to work in an irregular medium than if they had been faced with irregularity from the very beginning of reading instruction, as Chall (1967) suggests.

Though many E.S.N. schools and remedial centres report considerable success with i.t.a., research would seem to suggest that it is the bright child who gains proportionately more help from the medium if success is judged in terms of attainment. The intellectually dull child is usually helped into reading earlier by i.t.a. but apparently finds difficulty in the transfer to t.o. Burt (1967) has suggested that a reason for this may be a difference in the imagery patterns among children; bright children may be more able to cope adequately with auditory imagery than the dull who are predominantly visualisers. Thus the bright child would have a second advantage in that he could more readily appreciate and use phonics in his reading, whereas the dull child would be held back in his reading progress by a lower level of linguistic competence.

Further reading
DOWNING, J. A. (1967) *Evaluating the Initial Teaching Alphabet*. London: Cassell.
SCEATS, J. (1967) *i.t.a. and the Teaching of Literacy*. London: Bodley Head.
WARBURTON, F. W. and SOUTHGATE, V. (1969) *i.t.a. An Independent Evaluation*. London: Murray/Chambers.

USING COLOUR CODING

Words in Colour

Nellie Dale introduced colour as an aid to word recognition in the 1890s and colour has been used by some teachers and reading schemes ever since that time. Gattegno, however, was the first person to use a system of colour coding intended to give the whole of the language phonic regularity. His scheme, *Words in Colour*, which appeared in 1962, uses 41 colours. Each colour represents a sound no matter what letter or letters are used. Initially, the child learns to associate a speech sound with a colour but as the traditional spelling of the sound in that word is retained there is no great transfer problem. The system is of course only intended to be an aid to the early stages of reading and at all stages the child also has to work in normal black print.

Colour is used only on the twelve Fidel and twenty-one word

charts for group or class use and if the teacher wishes for blackboard work. In the books and worksheets traditional black print on white paper is used and the child does not use colour in his written work. The books, consisting of a *Word Building Book*, three readers and a *Book of Stories*, are not illustrated. A script type print is employed and, in the readers, punctuation is only gradually introduced and capital letters are absent. There is no attempt in the three readers to produce stories. They consist of odd phrases and sentences selected because they show steps in the growth of complexity of the spelling patterns of the English language.

The Fidel charts are Gattegno's analysis of all the spellings of the forty-one sounds of standard English and are hung on the wall for reference. The twenty-one word charts form part of the teaching equipment and Gattegno, using the five vowels on the first chart, intends that the children should master the following basic ideas:

1 Each sound has one corresponding sign and each sign one corresponding sound.
2 The sound is said as many times as it is written.
3 When signs (letters) are linked together they represent a shortening of time and pauses are shown by spaces between letters.

Thus the child is trained to respond to letters individually and in groups and the seeds of word and sentence reading are sown.

The first activity is termed by Gattegno 'visual dictation'. The child is introduced to the first vowel in the form 'This is the white one—it says "a".' The teacher will then use the first chart or the blackboard to get the children to respond orally to groups, for example:

a   aa   aaa   a   aaaa

When all the vowels have been introduced in a similar fashion the child will respond orally as the teacher points to letters in the following way:

aeu   iou   aeiu   oeiau

The first consonants to be introduced are 'p', 't' and 's'—an excellent choice, for the number of words which can be created is quite large. At first the child learns to join each vowel to a consonant, such as:

'ap'   'pa'   'ep'   'pe'
'at'   'ta'   'et'   'te'

29

The child now creates words from the sounds he knows, like at, ut, et, it, ot and decides which are real words. Next he can expand to three- and four-letter words, for example, pat, put, pet, tap, tip, top, stop, spot, pots. At this stage the child is encouraged to make sentences, for example, pip pats spot.

Over a period of time each sound is introduced by colour and at first by its most regular and common means of being represented by letter or letters. At every stage base words using the sound are suggested and the children are asked to supply other words and use them in sentences. A further activity which is used widely in the worksheets is turning one word into another by substituting a letter, adding a letter to any part of the word or inverting the letter order. The child can be asked to see how few moves are necessary, changing one letter only at a time or how many routes he can use to get to the required final word. More recently a selection of words has been produced on coloured card where the colours denote the part of speech. From these the child can learn the grammatical function of each word in the sentence.

The colour coding is based upon an excellent analysis of the sounds and spelling patterns of the English language. However, Gattegno has also produced a teaching method which is essential if any use is to be made of his work. The question of the relevance of both the method and the analysis to the way in which children learn to read must remain unanswered for the approach has attracted little attention from research workers.

The approach relies heavily on class or group instruction and drill type activities. The teacher therefore must keep children moving at a reasonably equal rate which would seem contrary to most normal practice at the infant stage. Again there is no suggestion that any pre-reading work should be done, the children apparently just start and, Gattegno claims, become fluent in as little as six weeks. There can be no doubt that children need help in listening to speech sounds and the ability to recognise sounds within words is essential to this approach. Working with eight- and nine-year-old children in remedial reading groups we found some children were not capable of using the approach because of a lack of development of their auditory perception. A further group found the approach distressing emotionally whilst some children made good progress. We have as yet not discovered a reliable means of deciding in advance of using the approach which children will be successful and which distressed.

The approach would seem contrary to many of the accepted principles of infant education for it is essentially teacher orientated and neglects the language and experience which young children bring to school with them. In other words, there is a danger of the reading process being divorced from reality and its role as a tool in widening the understanding of the child's environment. Gattegno has emphasised that the approach is a creative one but, in the early stages at least, it is creative, only in so far as the children are creating words and making sentences from them. The term creative is usually applied to the child's representation in language of experiences, thoughts and ideas and this would not be easy in the heavily structured manner in which the words are introduced according to the complexity of spelling pattern.

The approach requires a return to the timetabled reading lesson and though this might be excused if fluency was reached in six weeks our observations in infant schools have failed to produce any child who has achieved this. The use of colour seems extraordinarily complex for a five-year-old even allowing for the fact that it is never necessary for him to memorise all the colours in relation to the sounds represented. The materials lack intrinsic interest and vitality and the drills and artificiality might well induce word attack habits which might seriously impede the development of fluency at a later stage.

Although children who learn well with this approach seem to gain considerable independence in reading and discover a good deal about word and language structure they do not seem to acquire any better ability to comprehend than other children. The slower children observed did not appear to have gained much linguistic understanding when they eventually achieved the same level of attainment on word recognition tests as the brighter children.

The material in the three readers is most uninteresting—perhaps the best comment on it appears in Book 3, where Gattegno has written, 'the words pneumatic, plaque and obnoxious are only used by very few persons but I can read them'. A supply of some lively supplementary readers allied to the growth structure of the approach would considerably improve the material. The method is designed to encourage the discovery of the duties and sounds of letters and words which should lead to independence. It appears, however, that for many children the early words used must be practised and memorised before further growth can take place. The approach is felt to have more possibilities for the remedial field than the infant school stage.

Further reading
GATTEGNO, C. (1962) *Words in Colour: Background and Principles.* Reading: Educational Explorers.
A description of the rationale behind the *Words in Colour* approach.

MURPHY, M. L. (1968) *Douglas Can't Read*. Reading: Educational Explorers.
A case study of one child showing how progress was encouraged by use of *Words in Colour*.

Colour Story Reading

This scheme was devised by J. K. Jones and was the subject of a research programme organised by the London University Reading Research Unit from 1965 to 1967. The system uses only four colours, black, red, green and blue and nine background shapes so it is commended by its simplicity. The use of colour has however succeeded in drawing attention to the majority of difficulties involved in the sound symbol relationships of the English language.

There are significant differences in the use made of colour here from the use made by Gattegno. In Gattegno's system each colour always stands for the same sound but not so in *Colour Story Reading*. The short vowels are coloured either green or blue and the long vowels are always in red. Thus the 'a' in 'cat' is green and the 'o' in 'box' blue. The 'a' in 'acorn' and the 'o' in 'rope' would both appear in red. Thus the child is involved in a knowledge of phonic structure rather than simply relating a sound to a colour. The letter 'y' can be a long or short vowel or a consonant and therefore appears in different colours: red in 'tyre', blue in 'myth', green in 'yes'. The dipthongs 'oy', 'oi', 'ow' and 'ou' appear in green; thus the 'oi' in 'toil' would be green but in 'coincidence' the 'o' would be red and the 'i' blue.

The background shapes do however denote a sound whatever the spelling:

Blue	Green	Red
triangle 'sh' (she)	'oo' (good or could)	indeterminate vowel (the)
circle silent letters	'oo' (loose or blue)	'er' (her or purse)
square 'or' (four)	'ar' (jar or vase)	'air' (Chair or there)

The consonants again appear in three colours but the representation is colour and letter shape to sound not just colour and sound. Here Jones has helped identification by having 'b', 'd' and 'p' in different colours; 'p' as in 'pot' would be red but 'p' in 'sphere' would have the 'ph' in green, showing that it makes the 'f' sound which is itself green; 'g', 'x', 's' and 'c' appear in blue when they are hard as the 'g' in 'get', but red when soft as the 'g' in 'gem'.

Lastly, a 'non-conformist' symbol is used and this is simply a letter printed in black. Although Jones has given this section of his breakdown this name these symbols are in fact fairly regular.

'f' as in 'of'	'i' in 'Pauline'
's' as in 'pleasure'	'th' as in 'thick'—('th' in 'that' is red)
'x' in 'exact'	'e' in 'pretty'
'qu' in 'conquer'	'o' in 'some'
'n' or 'ng' in 'long'	'd' in 'jumped'

Less regular are the use of black for the 'u' in 'busy' and 'penguin' and for 'a' in 'any', 'cottage, and 'was'.

The teaching material consists of three short readers, a wall chart showing the colour system and a set of nineteen stories which can be obtained in book form for the teacher to read to the children or excellently presented on three long-playing records. The children's books are in fact a re-telling of the nineteen stories and are concerned with the introduction of the letters, sounds and colours. Like many modern approaches *Colour Story Reading* introduces a method along with the material. The child learns to listen to and isolate sounds in words and the character or characters which represent them. The colour helps to bridge the gap between the two as do the story characters who have names associated with the sounds and the children are taken on imaginary adventures with such people as 'ink', 'orange' and 'umbrella'.

The books themselves are rather slim and could be extended. Again the introductory work would have to be rewritten entirely for remedial work with older children if the approach is to be used to its best advantage. Colour is employed throughout the readers and there is the possibility that the children could become over dependent upon it. However the children's written work and some simple readers where colour is not used should guard against this possibility.

In some schools it appears that children are perhaps using colour in their written work too frequently. The use of four colours is exciting for the children in the early stages and can be retained with profit for the recording of new words in 'dictionaries', captions and charts, but is a hinderance to progress in creative writing. The use of the characterisation of the sounds opens up a wide field of creative and dramatic activity related to and helpful to reading progress. This type of work adds greatly to the enjoyment of reading activities, to the development of auditory discrimination and the relationship of sound to symbol.

Little suggestion is given for the use of the colour system beyond the early stages but it would help the child to have a personal dictionary where the various new words and rules he met could be classified on the basis of their sound values. Indeed a book based on the analysis of English spelling used by Gattegno using Jones' colour representation with sample words would be a most helpful document for the child. This would not only be a dictionary or spelling book but would form the basis for a growing knowledge of the phonetics of English and the relationship of these sounds to our spelling system. Another most useful document would be a book of rhymes which would readily explain the colour system and consolidate it. Nursery rhymes or the ones in Gertrude Baldwin's *Patterns of Sound* would be suitable.

One remedial clinic was observed where Jones' system was used as a partial aid but the results did not seem too encouraging. On the other hand, its retention as a partial aid after initial use of the material as a main scheme would seem desirable. We found that the approach had particular value with young junior school children who have not previously been successful in learning to read. The use of colour seemed to add not only a new logic to English which was understood by the child of low ability but the books are sufficiently different in presentation to seem a new process. Thus motivation was increased and success was more easily achieved. This would have been even greater if the material had been a little less 'childish' in content and somewhat more extensive.

In comparison to Gattegno's approach, *Colour Story Reading* cannot boast an equally exhaustive cueing system. It has inconsistencies, but these are more than compensated for by the way in which the system can be allied to the creative work of an infant school class. The bridging of the gap between sound and symbol by the use of stories as well as colour makes it easier for the child to overcome the inconsistencies of our spelling.

Further reading
JONES, J. K. (1965) 'Colour as an aid to visual perception in early reading.' *Br. J. educ. Psychol.* **35** (1), 22–7.
A description of a small research among nursery school children.
JONES, J. K. (1967) *Teacher's Manual. Colour Story Reading.* London: Nelson.

Reading by Rainbow

This scheme grew from the experience of two teachers within a school who felt that they had found an approach to the very early stages of reading which achieved very good results. The material designed for infants consists of four basic readers, two supplementary readers at Book 3 stage, reference cards which show the coloured letters and give illustrations to direct the child to the sound and worksheets where the child is given help to recognise letters.

Four colours are used; red, blue, yellow, and black. Red is used for long vowel sounds as 'a' in 'cake' and the 'ee' in 'deep'. Yellow is used for all silent letters which are described as 'magic' letters. Blue is used only for 'd' to distinguish it from 'b' and 'o' or 'oo' as in 'you' 'to' and 'loose'. Black is used for the short vowel sounds and the consonants other than 'd'. All words which cannot be analysed by the above aids are written in black and listed at the back of each book as 'look-say' words.

The use of four colours in this scheme is much less than in *Colour Story Reading* and on any page of the reader the child always meets far more black letters than all the other colours together. Thus there should not be any great transfer problem. Unlike the Jones's system there is really no attempt to regularise English but simply to provide a few phonic clues as a basis for aiding the child to use a traditional phonic approach. There is less likelihood of harmful 'learning sets' being created by a dependency upon the signalling system than with most other colour media, but this also means that the cueing system is less helpful.

The colour is attractive to the child and the grading of the introduction of sounds has been carefully worked out. The manual suggests a number of games, dramatic activities and group oral work aimed at the development of aural and visual discrimination. Development of these skills is essential to the approach, for the child must learn to decode and encode right from the beginning of the scheme. This, however, is inconsistent with the theory that a child must have attained the Piagetian stage of concrete operations before being able to decode (Piaget 1956).

We feel that this scheme is best used as a help to the development of phonic awareness among older infant and junior school children rather than as a central scheme for five-year-olds.

A Remedial Reading Method

Moxon (1962) has developed an admirable active approach to reading for children who have experienced failure. Though the major part of his work is concerned with the formulation of apparatus and games a brief description of the method is included here because he makes use of a colour code. This is rather different from the other approaches which have been described.

One of the main items of equipment is the 'Box of Letters'. The letters are printed in black on coloured cards and this background colour directs the child to the particular sound value or function of the letter. White card is used for the consonants, and the more difficult digraphs such as 'ch', 'sh', 'ph' and 'th', and the child refers to these as 'head' or 'tail' letters. Green card is used for the vowels or 'body' letters and Moxon suggests that these give the 'Go' signal for in tackling a new word the child is asked to look at the vowel before the consonants on either side of it. Red cards indicate the presence of special rules and therefore the child must stop and think. Red is used both for silent 'e' and any vowel it modifies. Red is also used for irregular sounds such as 'gh' or 'ought'. Blue card is used for common suffixes such as 'tion' and 'ed'. The child learns the sounds of the letters in his box by reference to charts in the four colours used. Here he locates the letter, lifts up a flap and discovers an explanatory picture which gives him the clue to the sound.

Moxon has produced an impressive number of machines, discs, charts, slides and posting boxes all of which are designed to teach a given phonic rule. He has built these into a continuous scheme during which the child will not only follow a course of phonic growth but also have the motivating influence of new items of apparatus. The apparatus has not been published but full directions for its manufacture are included in Moxon's own description of the scheme. Perhaps it is the extensive nature of the scheme and the time and effort necessary to produce the apparatus which has discouraged teachers from using it. Many schools and reading clinics have been observed using odd pieces of the apparatus but nowhere have we observed the complete scheme.

The approach is based on traditional phonic teaching and though the colour and apparatus bring interest and activity to the work, it is an aid to the development of primary reading skills only. The success of the child using the materials will be relative to his ability to analyse and synthesise. Consequently a good deal of oral work must be included. The manner suggested for the examination of new words seems rather clumsy—starting with the vowel, adding the final consonant and then putting in the initial letter. It may be a hinderance to speedy word recognition at a later stage and prevent the development of good directional attack.

Further reading
MOXON, C. A. V. (1962) *A Remedial Reading Method.* London: Methuen.
Contains a complete description of the Moxon approach plus detailed directions for the production of the machines and apparatus.

Wordmaster Major

It is obvious from the number of systems described that colour has attracted a good deal of attention in recent years. There is behind this move a fair amount of evidence that children respond more to colour than to shape and hence black print on white paper must seem rather uninteresting to them. In the majority of cases the use made of colour has been directed at simplifying the sound/symbol relationship of the language but in the *Wordmaster Major* colour is used simply to make the print more attractive and stimulating.

The designers of this equipment do not hope to replace any existing material but rather feel that they have produced a set of games whereby the child will be more highly motivated in his response to the printed word. The kit is composed of a number of cards where a variety of the most used words of the English language are printed in either green, red, blue or purple. The words are also printed in varying sizes but all in lower-case letters. The scheme uses 125 words and fourteen cards with twenty words on each. Each word appears therefore on either two or three of the cards. Every card has the same list of thirty 'joining' words and two 'jokers' at the foot of the page for when the material is being used for making up sentences. Two master sheets listing alphbetically all the words with the card numbers on which they appear and each individual card in colour are provided along with some suggested games.

All the games cannot be described here but the reader may gain some idea of the approach from the following:

1 *Word recognition—shape to shape*
Each child has a colour card and a number of blank slips of card. The teacher selects a word and writes it on the blackboard. If the child has the word on his card he covers it and then raises his hand so the teacher can check with the master sheet that he is correct or give further help if the child does not find the correct word.

2 *Sound to shape*
A similar procedure to the above but the teacher reads the word to the child rather than writing it.

3 *Sentences*
The children are given cards and asked to make sentences using the coloured words, the black joining words and no more than two 'joker' words (i.e. words of their own choice not represented

on the card). A pre-determined number of sentences are set and the winner is the first to reach this number.

The material has been in use in a number of ILEA schools for two years prior to publication and has been received quite enthusiastically. Children certainly seem to enjoy using the material but as is the case with all reading games it is very difficult to assess how much actual learning directly results from it. There is certainly more value here both in terms of interest and the variety of ways in which the material can be used than is found in the traditional use of flash cards or the more recent lotto games. It would probably be improved however if it were worked out more in stages and related directly to the vocabulary of, say, a reading scheme. (See also *English Colour Code* Tapes and Worksheets, page 45.)

Chapter 3 Phonic and Linguistic Approaches

At first sight it would seem strange that in an era when informality and child-centred education are the key-notes, the trend in the production of reading materials has been to emphasise the skills involved in word recognition. One of the reasons for this may be that it is felt that materials for reading should themselves incorporate the strategies and skills involved rather than that the working out of growth patterns should be left to the teacher. In addition, some research suggests that the possibility of success is somewhat higher when learning is carefully structured. During the first half of the twentieth century the majority of teachers employed a phonic type of approach in their reading teaching. A number of infant teachers still hold to a traditional approach to phonics, as is partly shown by the continuing sales of the Beacon readers. This scheme, first published in 1923, is still selling very well. The scheme has advantages other than its basically phonic structure for the later books still represent some of the best tellings of folk tales for children. The early books however show some of the difficulties of a narrow phonic approach not least of which is the difficulty of producing an interesting story and fluent English.

Traditional phonic approaches have lost popularity partly through the disenchantment of teachers with drill type activities and stilted texts but also as a result of evidence from, among others, Schonell (1949) and Piaget (1956) who have suggested that many children in the infant school have not reached the stage when they can work in a sufficiently abstract manner to undertake analysis and synthesis. Others of course consider the whole process rather pointless as it is virtually impossible for the young child to master the numerous rules he would need to learn in order to attack all words in his book with a phonic technique. Nevertheless the child is helped in attacking an unknown word if he can use a phonic technique and this aids the development of independence in reading. In view of this, authors and publishers have endeavoured to provide improved materials and some teachers have placed phonic work later in their teaching programme.

A cursory glance at a test which professes to owe its origins to linguistic studies may well leave the impression that a linguistic approach is nothing more than a new name for a traditional phonic approach. Indeed, even among many of the authors of such schemes there appears to be no clear idea of a distinction between the two. Some basically linguistic approaches bear titles which contain the word phonic within them. In a pure linguistic approach the reading material is structured so that children can learn the value of each letter within a whole-word context and are not required to respond to letters by producing isolated letter sounds. A second major difference between phonic and linguistic methods lies in the origin of the steps to be learned. In phonics a sequence and set of rules have grown up over the years on a trial and error basis derived from practice. In linguistic methods, spelling patterns are graded with regard to their complexity. Children are thus asked to respond to spelling patterns rather than to simple letter-sound relationships.

Further reading
MERRITT, J. E. (1968) 'The Linguistic Approach to Reading.' In DOWNING, J. A. and BROWN, A. L. (eds.) *Third International Reading Symposium*. London: Cassell.
A brief and concise description of opposing views on the contribution of linguistics to the teaching of reading.

Fun with Phonics

This scheme represents the efforts of a Cambridgeshire teacher, C. V. Reis, to produce activities with a strong play element which would make the learning of the major phonic rules effective and enjoyable. A range of apparatus and a handbook containing suggestions for games and further activities resulted from this work. The kit is not an attempt to provide a reading scheme but is intended as supplementary work to be used alongside any reading scheme.

The first item in the kit is a set of 'Hanging Cards'—large coloured pieces of card each with one letter upon it. Vowels appear on yellow card, red for easily confused letters (for example b, p, d) and green for the remaining consonants. These cards have cords attached and children hang them round their necks and come together in groups to form words or in two's to form digraphs. An introductory game (*My fair lady*) is played with these cards to gain letter/sound recognition. Throughout the scheme posting activities play a large part. The posting boxes consist of folded card with a slot in the front. The early boxes have a picture and the initial letter of the object portrayed on them. Individual letters are provided on eight different coloured cards so that each child can have his own colour and the teacher can check which children are successful or are having difficulties. In Stage 2 the post boxes each have a picture but no letter printed on them. As each child masters one group of letters he progresses to the next group.

Workbooks involving templates are employed. The child is given a letter and selects a template of an object whose name commences with this letter. He draws the outline and colours his picture with crayon, finally copying the given letter. At a later stage the child is given a group of templates and must write in his own letters without help, moving on later to writing words and sentences. There are pictures and letter cards for matching activities, and games and further posting activities for various groups of sounds and words and a set of cards for 'Family Snap'. Lastly, the complete kit has a flash card 'Twirler'.

In all, it is an extensive scheme. There are for example over 300 posting boxes and some 2 700 small slips of card. Thus the teacher must be most efficient in her organisation if she is to keep all the material ready for use. The posting boxes themselves are rather flimsy, take up rather a lot of room when in use and are easily blown over by the slightest draught which makes accurate checking of the children's work difficult. The Twirler aims to prevent movement as the teacher holds up a flash card. However though it eliminates horizontal movement the vertical movement of the word may well bring in reversal problems. The material is well schemed from the point of view of a phonic approach and certain sections of it can prove most helpful to the infant teacher.

Programmed Reading Kit

This material was prepared experimentally by D. H. Stott during the period 1954 to 1962 with the help of a group of teachers and drew on a number of ideas for apparatus put forward by Ronald Morris. As a result of his previous work with retarded children Stott was convinced that one of the major stumbling blocks to reading progress was a lack of phonic skills. He felt, however, that to undertake such work in book form inevitably resulted in stilted uninteresting text or far too steep a gradation of difficulty.

Stott set out, therefore, to devise a set of materials which would impart phonic knowledge and encourage the growth of phonic skills and yet at the same time be independent of reading books. As there was not to be any story element to catch the child's interest the material was organised into individual and group games which are largely self-corrective. The kit does not therefore replace reading books but would normally be used alongside them. In the case of children who have a long history of failure

41

with more traditional approaches however it is sometimes helpful to use the kit alone for a while to gain improved attitudes towards reading. Space does not permit a full description of all the games and activities but those described below will give the reader some idea of the nature of the materials.

The first stage in the kit consists of the 'Group Game' with the Morris Cards for older children and the Touch Cards for younger children. The Group Game is of the domino type. The cards are folded with a picture on the inside and a letter on the outside. Each player sets his cards up in front of him so that he can see the pictures but the other players can only see the letters. One player calls out the name of an object illustrated on one of his cards. The other players then try to identify the card by attending to the initial sound and associating it with the sound of one of the letters which they can see on the reverse side of the caller's cards. If a child makes the correct selection he then takes the card. If not, he is not allowed to have a second chance immediately, which discourages hit and miss guessing. The Touch Cards are also designed to help the child to appreciate the sound of initial letters in words and to relate them to printed symbols. The children listen to the teacher who says one of two words, for example 'monkey' or 'spade'. Then the child touches the appropriate picture. When he is proficient with the picture cards the same procedure is used with letter cards.

The 'Brick Wall Game' assists the child to build up simple phonic words. An 'umpire' is used to check that a true word has been made by referring to his dictionary card. The materials consist of brick-shaped pieces of card which have the beginning section of words at the right-hand edge and final letters at the left-hand edge. The child fits them together building a wall which results only in complete words.

The value of reading games in promoting reading growth has often been questioned. The *Programmed Reading Kit* is predominantly game material but it is more extensive and more carefully graded than the majority of reading games so that used well it has a greater possibility of effecting reading improvement than an isolated reading game. On the other hand its title is misleading—it is graded rather than programmed and it is phonic work not reading. The teacher will need to play a very active role in its use if it is to teach rather than merely consolidate work already covered. Again it is essential that other reading work goes on alongside so that meaning is also used as an aid to word recognition, otherwise the child could be reduced to having to analyse each successive word in his reader. Stott saw this difficulty and, realising that 180 of the 250 most common words suggested by McNally and Murray (1962) did not conform to the more simple phonic rules, introduced a set of books and games intended for teaching these words (*Day of the Week Books*).

Daniels and Diack (1956) consider the sounding of letters to be far too abstract an activity during the early stages of reading. Stott however builds a system of word analysis and synthesis into his scheme. He feels it essential that in a three letter word the child should link together the first consonant and the vowel whereas most teachers link the vowel to the final consonant. Gattegno on the other hand suggests the child must always link a vowel to every consonant and teaches the child to work with both 'ap' and 'pa'.

The Stott material is being widely used in remedial work and has found its way into the normal class situation. But much of the value of this extensive scheme is frequently lost because few teachers seem to use all the materials in a regular progression. Used as a whole with regularity it can be useful but there are some children who tire of the games or find difficulty in relating the work within the Kit to the normal reading situation. Recently we have observed a number of infant schools using the kit and though some teachers seem to think highly of it, we feel that some of the activities are not really suited to the infant school child. The great emphasis on phonic analysis in some of the material may cause difficulties for the children later on. Though the material was designed originally for secondary children it seems to work best and be most enjoyed by the slower readers in the junior school. Dr Stott has been working on a revision of the kit which will be available shortly.

Further reading
STOTT, D. H. (1964) *Roads to Literacy*. Glasgow: W. & R. Holmes. A presentation of the rationale upon which the kit was based and a description of the materials.

Phonic Tapes—Remedial Supply Company

This scheme was the first extensive taped scheme to be available commercially. It was originally worked out by teachers in the remedial situation but has also been observed in use in infant schools. It consists of three seven-inch tapes, workbooks, a letter tray and sheets of letters. It aims to provide complete phonic training through all the more common phonic rules and includes listening, identification, oral analysis and synthesis as well as the building of words from the card letters supplied and the completion of exercises in the workbooks.

In common with all taped phonic schemes each teacher will feel it necessary to re-record sections where there are distinct dialect differences. It is felt that in this particular scheme there is an unnecessary amount of switching the player on and off which not only breaks concentration but also wastes a lot of valuable space on the tape. The tapes assume the child has some knowledge of print and of the names of letters. This use of name and sound together is questionable for it can lead the child into a state of confusion between the two. Further, the early rules are given in such a way as to suggest that they are universal and this can make it more difficult for the child to face the irregularities of English at a later date.

Clifton Audio-Visual Reading Programme

This scheme consists of two tapes, forty reading cards, workbooks and a test card. The publishers have been somewhat over-ambitious in their title for it is not a 'reading programme'. It deals exclusively with phonics not total reading and though its format and grading are closely allied to a linear programme it does not fulfil the requirements of programming in the smallness of its steps and the way in which answers follow logically from the material presented.

If it is accepted as a graded phonic scheme it is easier to understand and has a greater possibility for valid use. The scheme was developed within the framework of remedial education and so is not really suitable for operation in the infant class. Children needing extra individual help in phonics at the junior or secondary stage may derive great benefit from it.

A diagnostic test card is provided which gives the teacher the information necessary to ensure that the child commences work within the scheme at the most appropriate point. The tapes are used in conjunction with the reading cards and supply oral phonic practice and experience in the relationship of sound and symbol. The worksheets are allied to each stage and provide written practice of the work undertaken on tape. We would suggest that further work in other phonic schemes is helpful and one school where it was used in conjunction with Stott's *Programmed Reading Kit* (1964) seemed to be gaining considerable success. Short periods of work within the scheme are recommended because the programme-type approach soon becomes boring for children and it is necessary to give time for the knowledge gained to be consolidated by use before the number of items becomes too large.

English Colour Code Worksheets and Tapes

This scheme has been worked out by Moseley as part of his work at the Centre for Learning Disabilities. It is probably the most carefully researched scheme to have been produced to date. The words used have been obtained from a study of many words lists compiled from children's literature, conversation and writing. The order of the introduction of letter/sound combinations does not simply follow the pattern which has grown up by tradition but has been based on an immense computer study in America (Hodges and Rudorf 1965) which estimated the frequency of occurrence of all sound/symbol patterns in English. Those most frequently occurring are introduced in the early part of the scheme. This gives the child a greater command of the language and a better chance to use the skills learned to cope with other words. A system of colour cues is used on the worksheets to introduce each new sound and to give extra help in recognition and association of spelling patterns.

There are two tapes and sixty worksheets. The tapes are used to introduce and guide the work undertaken on the worksheets. They are presented in a lively manner and employ realistic sound effects and rhymes. Both sustain interest and the rhymes are a further stimulus for helping the child to memorise the sounds being taught. The worksheets have illustrations and rhymes as well as written exercises for the child to complete. The most notable feature in this scheme, however, is the manner of presentation. The cards, despite the fact that the children write on them, are non-consumable. They have been coated with a surface which is washable and even writing in ball-point pen can be cleaned off without trace.

The scheme is aimed entirely at the improvement of phonic skills and has been developed in and for remedial work. It is not really suitable for infants but is probably the most attractive and effective taped approach to phonics for remedial work. It is just a little disappointing that the written exercises are somewhat traditional and stereotyped when so much good work has gone into all other aspects of the approach.

THE PHONIC-WORD METHOD

After the Second World War a good deal of criticism was made of currently accepted theories behind the teaching of reading and of the standards which were being achieved by British children. In America a movement grew up which has come to be known as the 'Phonic Revolt'. Flesch (1955), as one of its leaders, produced his book *Why Johnny Can't Read* which advocated a return to highly formal tuition and phonic drills. A similar movement in Britain proved to be somewhat more constructive and from the dissatisfactions expressed Daniels and Diack (1956) produced the phonic-word approach which was later embodied in their *Royal Road* reading scheme.

In the early 1950s it was the vogue to teach reading by the 'whole-word' method and most infant teachers at that time would profess that they were teaching reading by a look-say or sentence method. Daniels and Diack criticised not only the whole-word methods but also traditional approaches to phonic work.

Whole-word methods were attacked because they ignored the fact that individual letters have a definite part to play in word recognition and that it is virtually impossible for a child to recognise a word by its outline shape. It was stressed that such methods encouraged guesswork and careless reading habits and could in fact over a period of time lessen a child's undoubted ability to recognise minor differences in letter shapes. The selection of words on the basis of their contrasting shapes made for very stilted early readers and interest among the children could be killed by the high rate of word repetition which was necessary in an attempt to gain memorisation.

The traditional phonic approach was equally criticised. Daniels and Diack believed that the sounding out of letters did not give the child the ability to blend them into the original word. For the child the sounds 'c—a—t' do not make 'cat' because consonants cannot really be efficiently sounded alone. Thus the relationship is an abstract one which can only be built up as a result of long experience and maturity. For the child, the sounds 'ker-a-ter' do not make 'cat' however quickly the separate sound are uttered. Like whole-word approaches the traditional phonic approach resulted in unrealistic, dull and limiting reading books and the child's interest in reading would be further sapped by long sessions of uninspiring drill and repetition.

Daniels and Diack established three principles upon which reading materials should be based.

1 The materials should be well illustrated and involve the child in an active manner.

2 They should sustain the interest of the children.

3 They should lead the children step by step, but as rapidly as possible, to an understanding that letters in words stand for sounds in a certain order and should begin by teaching the child the most common sound values of the letters.

Daniels and Diack devised an approach which would satisfy these criteria and which would capitalise on the advantages of both 'whole' and phonic approaches yet avoid their pitfalls. In the early stages the child uses card apparatus to link simple words to pictures. These are grouped to emphasise a given sound within each word. For example the child will meet 'top', 'tap', 'tin' and 'tub' and his attention will be drawn to the sound 't' which they have in common. Thus the letter sounds are always presented in the first instance as an integral part of the word and the child is led by the structuring of the material into a knowledge of the duty and sound value of the letter. The child will over a period of time meet this letter in various positions in words and be asked to supply the missing symbol to complete a word with the help of an illustration. This unites the child's visual and aural experience. Although the child is requested to supply orally other words which he knows that have the 't' sound no attempt is made at this time to introduce the reading of such words as 'true' and 'table' which the child will no doubt supply. These words introduce more advanced phonic rules and in the early stages of teaching we believe that only words which use the most common sounds of all their component letters should be used. A careful analysis of the spelling patterns of the language has been produced and the scheme introduces the various steps in phonic complexity at a controlled rate. Daniels and Diack realised that the irregularity of our language militates against a thorough-going phonic approach. In order to sustain the child's interest by providing attractive story material they introduce words into their readers such as 'here' and 'what' as look/say words. Many such words will of course be explained by phonic rules which the child will learn at a later stage.

The method was embodied in the *Royal Road* readers which appeared in 1956 after preliminary experimentation with non-readers in the junior school. The readers do not match up to our criteria of 'good illustration' and the pages seem overcrowded with words in the first two books. They do however involve the child in activity and from the earliest stages the child is given work which requires not only a knowledge of the letter and sound structure of the words but also the ability to understand what has been read.

Although carefully ordered the grading of the books appears rather steep, especially at the infant school stage, and the child must be given carefully chosen supplementary material if he is to progress satisfactorily. The early books provide the material necessary for steady growth of the knowledge of phonic rules but at the later stages the teacher must take over this duty or new steps forward may be taken without the conscious knowledge which would lead to a generalisation of the rule for use when meeting it in other words. It is essential that the child should come to the stage of making these inductive generalisations in respect of all the rules met, otherwise he may gain a limited knowledge of sounds and letters without acquiring a technique of allying one to the other. The teacher is also advised to devise activities for the efficient learning of the look-say words before they are met in the text or they can become quite a stumbling block to progress.

Jeanne Chall (1967) has suggested that a modified 'linguistic' approach (considered next in this chapter) plus 'language experience' work may be the most helpful method in the early stages of reading. Many of the books written for 'linguistic' approaches are very limiting but in the *Royal Road Readers* Daniels and Diack have produced what is virtually a modified linguistic approach. This has been achieved by the use of a controlled analysis of the sound/symbol relationship of words in the language plus the introduction of a small number of words which though irregular at this stage, enable the writer to produce reasonable story material. The *Royal Road Readers* are more suitable for juniors than infants but the method upon which they are based can be employed effectively with very young children.

Further reading
DANIELS, J. C. and DIACK, H. (1956) *Progress in Reading*. Nottingham: University Institute of Education.
Contains a description of the phonic-word method and the results of experimental trials.
DIACK, H. (1960) *Reading and the Psychology of Perception*. Nottingham: Peter Skimmer.
Argues the case for the use of the phonic-word method.

LINGUISTIC APPROACHES

A linguistic approach resembles the older phonic approaches in that only the more regular spellings of the sounds of the language are introduced in the early stages. A growth pattern based on spelling complexity is determined and in the purest form of the approach no word is used which does not conform to the rules already covered. A brief explanation of the method as described by Fries (1962) will serve to show the way in which linguistic approaches differ from traditional phonic approaches.

Fries's divisions of reading growth

Fries (1962) suggests that reading growth can be divided into three stages.

1 *The transfer stage*
Fries maintains that the basis of reading skill lies in the ability to make high speed responses to the visual presentation of letters. This therefore sets the first step, to enable the child to recognise, and discriminate between, letters. This is an entirely visual process at this stage, so letter names are dismissed as being totally unimportant, letter sounds as having little value due to the irregularity of our language and writing as a secondary skill as yet unnecessary. The child is required to work through recognition exercises and matching games starting with capital letters without serifs introduced in strict order of their mode of construction. All straight line letters are used first and those involving curved lines last. The child is presented with pairs of letters and has to say whether they are the same or different and then progresses to lists where like letters are joined by a line:

for example I   T
               T   T
               I   I
               T   I
               F   T
               E   F
               F   E
               T   F

When the child has mastered single letters, he begins to match pairs of letters, and finally words are introduced. It is at this latter stage that sound is used for the first time and the teacher says the words before the children work on matching and discrimination exercises with words. There is never any suggestion that the child should endeavour to split the words into their components sounds. Having gained some facility here, the use of lower-case letters and of sentences is begun. All the words employed however are strictly controlled by the extent of their spelling complexity. Families of words with similar patterns are built up and also the child practises speedy response to words with very similar spellings but different sounds:

for example MAN   MANE   MEAN
               FAT   FATE   FEAT

Fries not only insists on a rigid structure on the basis of spelling patterns but also stresses that the words used should be those within the linguistic experience of the child. This proviso would also hold good later, for the grammatical structure of sentences used. In the preparation of materials the order of words is carefully programmed so that any new item is tied by a simple contrast to an item previously practised:

for example   AT–CAT
CAT–RAT
AT–CAT–RAT–PAT
PAT A RAT
PAT A CAT
RAT–FAT–PAT
A FAT CAT   A FAT RAT
PAT RAT BAT
BAT A FAT RAT

At no stage however is the child to be asked what any given letter says. The unit of sound is always a complete word. This type of approach is used to explore all the major and some of the minor spelling patterns of the language. Fries suggests that this work takes between five hundred and a thousand hours of instruction depending on the child's abilities.

2   *Productive reading*
When the child has come to the stage where, without thinking, he can substitute visual symbols for the auditory signs of the spoken language he is able to attend only to meaning. The next step forward is to gain maximum meaning from the printed word. Fries asserts that the graphics of written English are insufficient to carry the full weight of emphasis and intonation that are present in the spoken word. He suggests therefore that early in the transfer stage the child should begin directed oral reading. Consequently as he progresses into this second stage his ability to produce appropriate stress and intonation patterns which give evidence of total understanding can be furthered. At certain stages the child will be asked to practice reading passages where stress marks have been added but the teacher is advised never to allow a child to read a sentence with less expression than would be used when speaking to a companion.

This stage is termed 'productive' in contrast to the transfer stage where the child is practising a receptive art. Here he is being asked to reproduce the full meaning of a given text by the maximum use of his own powers of expression in speech. All of this means that the child must also achieve a deep understanding of the material read and also something of the author's purpose in writing it.

3 *Vivid imaginative realisation*
This stage commences when the child can use a written text with as much freedom and ease as he can his own speech when exploring his environment. Here Fries is concerned with the 'literary' rather than the utilitarian aspects of reading. The child should now be helped to read in a way which will help him to relive the past experiences of others and gain something of their emotions and values. This will not only add to the level of his own internal understanding but deepen his insight and sensitivity to the more abstract areas of thought.

Fries has embodied the approach outlined above in a set of semi-programmed workbooks and readers known as the *Merrill Linguistic Readers* (1966). A cursory glance at them shows that he has held to his theoretical principles with regard to spelling patterns to a very high degree. This is achieved unfortunately at the cost of a content which appears stilted and unreal. There is a good deal of evidence which would indicate the importance of providing reading material in which the language patterns resemble those which the child himself habitually uses (Ruddell 1965).

Fries has emphasised that there must be complete meaning responses from the very beginning but such sentences as 'a cat at bat' hardly seem to fulfil this criteria. One may wonder, too, whether children really find the supposed humour funny or whether it appears ridiculous to them. The words used, though they may well be written within the average child's linguistic experience, will surely not have been used in the manner employed by Fries. Again the omission of many words most used in speech and in the mass of children's literature available adds to the unrealistic nature of the text so the child is not able to gain quick independence in reading by transferring his skill to other materials in his environment.

A structured approach has much to offer in security and steady growth but here the approach would seem to be overstructured with the added danger of giving the child the idea that our language follows completely regular rules. Chall (1967) has suggested that a child has greater difficulty with the irregular spellings of our language if all his early reading is done with material consisting only of regular words. Some of the irregularities should be introduced from the very beginning. Finally the very long period of work with very formal exercises and unrealistic texts might well result in destroying the child's interest so that he is prevented from reaching the ideals expressed under the headings of 'Productive reading' and 'Vivid imaginative realisation'.

The sentence as the linguistic unit

Most of the work upon reading which owes its origin to linguistics has emphasised either the sound/symbol relationship or the visual appreciation of the spelling patterns of the language. Lefevre (1964) takes a rather different point of view. Just as Jagger (1929) urged that all reading should be based on sentences, because only sentences express ideas from the point of view of child-centred education, so Lefevre brings forward the same idea from the linguistic standpoint. He feels that the individual word has no function until it is embodied in a sentence and that it can only be studied in relation to its grammatical function and its contribution to the total meaning. He suggests that the sentence should form the basic unit of reading instruction but fails to tell the teacher how this can be achieved. Reading is pointless unless the text conveys meaning to a child but it would be extremely difficult to gain reading independence for a child unless both words and letters as well as sentences are given some attention.

Further reading
FRIES, C. C. (1962) *Linguistics and Reading.* New York: Holt, Rinehart and Winston.
A description of Fries' approach.
LEFEVRE, C. (1964) *Linguistics and the Teaching of Reading.* New York: McGraw-Hill.

Programmed Reading

This series of books by Cynthia Buchanan is from the 'linguistic' stable and the approach has many similarities to that of Fries. However, the author terms her method a 'Visuo-phonic' approach and, as she does place some emphasis upon the function of the individual letter sound to the sound of the word, she also has something in common with the phonic-word method of Daniels and Diack.

The main section of the approach is based on programmed workbooks, even at the pre-reading stage. During this pre-reading stage the author intends that the child should master the following points:
1 The names of the letters of the alphabet.
2 How to print all the capital and small letters.
3 That letters stand for sounds.
4 The sound associated with the letters a, f, m, n, p, t, the and i (these form the basis of the work in the first programmed reader).
5 That letters are read from left to right.

6 That groups of letters form words.

7 How to read the words 'yes' and 'no' and the sentences:

> I am an ant;   I am a man;   I am a mat;   I am a pin;
> I am a pan;   I am tan;   I am thin;   I am fat.

This work is achieved through a number of lessons directed by the teacher and then consolidated by the Programmed Primer. The Primer is used under the teacher's guidance and therefore must be done as class or group work. A short test is given after this work to ensure that the child is ready to move on to the first series of books of the Programmed Reading Scheme.

There are three series of books in the Programmed Reading Scheme and each series consists of seven programmed workbooks and seven matched readers, a teacher's guide and book of tests. Each section of the programme is followed by a test. Throughout the books the text is allied to a meaningful picture. The child makes his response to each sentence, then checks his answer against the correct response which is revealed as he moves his slider down the page to reveal the next frame. The tests occur after every fifty or so frames—there are eight such tests in Book One. At the end of the first series a cumulative vocabulary of 1 400 words is reached and the child has been given work-attack skills which permit him to decode many more words.

In the second and third stages the vocabulary is consistently enlarged and comprehension is formally introduced. The scheme ends with what is claimed to be the world's first programmed novel. Here the device of fading words is used to extend knowledge of the sound rules and each body of text is followed by frames which test retention and comprehension. It is professed that by the end of the third series a child will have learned the whole sound/symbol system of the English language and will be able to read any new word presented to him. It is also suggested that the re-inforcement supplied by the programmed approach will have resulted in the child feeling that reading is a 'wonderful adventure'.

In comparison with Fries' approach the scheme is not quite so rigid in its adherence to a pre-conceived introduction of words according to spelling pattern, but even so the introduction of a small number of sight words has not been sufficient to remove the stilted nature of the text. After many months of work the child will be reading stories of which the following is an example.

'The hat is tan, the sand is tan and the ant is tan.
Sam is standing on his hat.
The ant stings him.
Sam has his tan hat.'

Such limitations are of course part of the whole approach. One peculiar example which arises and which must be very limiting for the child when he wants to read outside the scheme is that during the whole of Series One which supplies a vocabulary of 1 400 words the child will only meet the letter 'o' in the sight words 'on', 'no', 'to' and 'of'. The letter 'u' likewise does not appear until the seventh reader in Series One is used.

It can be seen therefore that there are difficulties in relating the programme to all the other work of the classroom and to the child's normal speech patterns. It is felt however that Buchanan has come a little nearer to achieving this than has Fries. One final criticism is that the workbooks are consumable and will prove very expensive at 70p to 85p if they are used in the manner intended.

The great value of such texts would seem to be their method of providing and ordering the spelling patterns of the language. The teacher is then helped and enabled to use this knowledge to increase the reading efficiency of the child. If the material takes over the whole learning situation however, an unreal reading environment is created whereby reading does not seem as vital a part of life as it could to the child.

Breakthrough to Literacy

This scheme is the first major attempt since the work of Daniels and Diack (1956) to incorporate the work in the field of linguistics into reading materials in Britain. This is rather surprising when one notes how many schemes based in linguistics have been produced in America in recent years. The material is the result of the research of a team working in the Department of General Linguistics at the University College London under a grant from the Schools Council.

The material produced consists of a blend of language experience and linguistic approaches. The work is meant to be based partly in the language suggested by the child and partly on words selected for the complexity of their spelling patterns. Though a number of books have been produced, these are not really graded readers and the major part of the work is based on the Sentence and Word Makers of the scheme.

Reading work commences by the teacher working with a group of children using two pieces of apparatus, a Magnet Board and the Teacher's Sentence Maker. The Magnet Board is accompanied by a number of figurines and the children are invited to supply words, sentences and stories about the people and things depicted. Labels made up of the children's language can then be attached to the board. The teacher uses her own Sentence Maker—a larger version of that which the children will use later—to show the beginning of written language, making use of the children's own names and sentences which they supply. At the same time the teacher must provide particular words and types of sentence structure which will ensure growth in language usage.

Once the child's interest in written language is stimulated he is given his own Sentence Maker. This is a folder containing a number of words arranged in pockets and blank cards so that the child can add his own personal words. The words supplied have been compiled from those which all children seem to know at the five to six years stage and represent the major spelling patterns of English. The child now experiments with the making of sentences, reads them, compares work with his fellows and eventually writes his own first reading book.

When the child needs help in discrimination among symbols he commences work with his Word Maker. This is a further folder containing letters on pieces of card. Here he builds words from the letters and the teacher will guide his attention towards new words and the function of the symbols in any given word.

The basic idea behind the construction of the scheme would seem to be an excellent one. Most of the important features for an effective start on reading seem to be present. The child supplies most of the actual language, it is an active and realistic approach and there is opportunity for each child to learn in the manner most appropriate to his abilities. In this respect there is rather more freedom for both teacher and child than one finds in a traditional reading scheme. The manual also supplies an excellent description of the spelling rules of English but it seems rather a pity that some detailed suggestions are not given as to the best order of their introduction to children. The teacher will therefore have to supply such a structure in line with the knowledge gained from previous experience of the needs of children, otherwise the approach may fall down owing to a lack of structure. The early stages seem to be well catered for but the teacher must ensure that a good foundation is followed up by an adequate growth pattern.

Further reading
MACKAY, D., THOMPSON, B. and SCHAUB, P. (1970) *Breakthrough to Literacy: Teacher's Manual.* London: Longmans.

Chapter 4   The Laboratory Approach to Reading

The growth of reading laboratories stems directly from the emphasis given to individual work as the most vital factor in reading development. Parker (1963) has suggested that in exchanging 'traditional' education for 'progressive' education we have thrown the baby out with the bath water. He suggests that the traditional situation was completely involved in the acquisition of skill or knowledge whilst the progressive movement has failed to provide the child with the skills needed to take advantage of active, realistic educational experiences. Thus Parker describes education as a two-fold process, namely 'skill-getting' and 'skill-using'. It is suggested that a base programme should be provided where skills are learned which can then be practised in creative and life-like situations.

When the first reading laboratories became available in the mid 1950s they were in some senses much more revolutionary in the U.S.A. than in England. English teachers had accepted a much more individual approach to learning than their American counterparts and were not hampered by the American interpretation of educational equality as meaning 'everyone having the same work at the same time'. On the other hand the area which appeared most revolutionary in England, namely the teaching of reading skills to a very high level, was already accepted in American theory if not carried out in practice.

Maximum learning takes place when a child starts from his existing level of competence and is allowed to move as far and as fast as he is capable. Laboratories seek to give the child this opportunity by careful placing and working on small self-corrected assignments. By very careful grading of the sub-skills involved in reading as well as the vocabulary, language structure and concepts present in the material the teacher is released for more individual work and can act as a 'learning consultant' and 'curriculum planner'.

The teacher must see laboratories in the light of the 'skill-getting' and 'skill-using' processes. Also the skills practised at each stage in the laboratory must be known. This is essential for the child will not automatically use a new skill outside the laboratory unless he is shown its relevance and helpfulness to his creative or project work or other reading. Well used, the laboratory should start a progression where the child learns a skill which enables him to undertake more advanced work. This in its turn suggests further skills which will be helpful to further his expertise. The construction of the laboratories is based on the behavioural sciences. A stimulus-response, reinforcement and redirection approach is implicit in the material. As such the material might well be classified as 'semi-programmed' or at least a very close relative of programmed learning but one which involves perhaps a more obviously active and challenging approach than the typical programme.

Whilst feeling that such an approach is helpful from the age of seven onwards we have reservations with regard to its use with children of infant school age. It is felt that at this stage the constant interaction of personality and the giving of adult approval and encouragement must play a very much greater part in the learning situation. Young children do not seem to respond as readily to 'things' as to people. Again a certain amount of independence and maturity is necessary if the child is to be able to gain not only from practice but also from his mistakes.

Further reading
MERRITT, J. E. (1967) 'The S.R.A. Laboratories.' In BROWN, A. L. (Ed.) *Reading: Current Research and Practice*. London: Chambers.
PARKER, D. H. (1963) *Schooling for Individual Excellence*. New York: Nelson.

Science Research Association Reading Laboratories

The first reading laboratory was produced by Dr D. H. Parker in the United States and his series of eleven reading laboratories is still the most extensive available.

Laboratory 1 is a series of word games through which the child learns the phonic skills involved in reading. It is not intended however that this laboratory be used in isolation but rather as a supplement to the work undertaken in the other laboratories. Thus the child will use the word games as long as his teacher feels this is necessary to the full development of his reading ability.

Children need the attainment and ability of the average six-year-old in order to commence work in the first laboratory of the series and from that point the whole growth of reading attainment is covered by the laboratories right up to the superior adult level of college and university students. The ten laboratories after the first have a common approach. All the reading material is graded from the point of view of vocabulary, growth of linguistic structure and the level of concepts normally achieved at that stage in reading. Again the type and difficulty of the exercises are graded and structured in an attempt to gain growth of the various sub-skills involved in reading.

The material within the laboratories falls under three headings —Power Builders, Rate Builders and Listening Skills. The Power Builders are divided into sections which are graded by colour and all the cards within a section practise the same skills and are of approximately the same reading standard. Each section represents a growth in comprehension attainment of four to six months though there is some variation here from one laboratory to another. Each Power Builder has an illustration followed up by a story and follow-up questions are set under two headings. The first of these is 'How well did you read?' and is aimed at accurate comprehension. The ability to evaluate the content and have insight into the author's purpose is stressed throughout the laboratories.

The second section 'Learn about words' contains a wide variety of work-study exercises and phonic work based on the text, which have a consistent growth pattern throughout the whole series. For each Power Builder there is a matched Rate Builder. These are short passages which the child must read and upon which he must answer questions within three minutes. The questions demand mainly a literal understanding of the passage. The listening skills are passages which are read to the pupils in the class who then answer questions about them.

The answers to the questions are recorded on specially prepared pages in the child's own record book. The questions in all sections ask for either a one word answer or a letter denoting which of a number of given alternatives the child feels is correct. The child marks his own work from answer keys, completes any corrections necessary and then with the aid of a table to convert his raw score to a percentage completes a histogram for each section of the work which readily shows both child and teacher the success which is being achieved. The record books also contain a starter-level test which enables the teacher to ensure that the child commences introductory work and work within the laboratory at the most appropriate point. In the later laboratories this introductory work consists mainly in explaining the approach and providing a sample Power Builder but in the earlier laboratories much more extensive teacher-guide work is included.

The laboratories are backed by an extensive range of other materials such as spelling laboratories and the Pilot Library readers. However, the reading laboratories were not originally intended to replace reading schemes, reading for pleasure and creative written work but rather to complement them.

Dr Parker himself suggests that the best results are obtained if the laboratories are used as 'booster' programmes one term in three. This would involve two or three forty-five-minute sessions per week over a twelve-week term. In each week a child would complete from two to five Power Builders, the same number of Rate Builders and one of the Listening Skill exercises. Few children seem to find it necessary to work through more than eight of the twelve Power Builders in order to move up to the next section and be successful in it.

Many experiments (for example Moyle 1966, Pont 1966) have shown that by using the 'booster' principle, average gains of a year or more in comprehension attainment may be achieved. This only seems to happen, however, on the first acquaintance with the laboratories. We conducted an experiment where work was carried out within a laboratory for one term per year throughout the four years in the junior school. An average growth for the four terms when SRA was used was nine months per term or twice the normal growth rate. There was a slight fall below the normal growth rate in the eight terms when the laboratory was not used, but on leaving the junior school the class concerned had an average comprehension age some thirteen months in advance of their mental age and only one child had a comprehension age below his mental age.

Observing the above situation would suggest that the resultant gains could be higher. This could be achieved by the teacher carefully studying the errors made by the children rather than simply accepting corrections and also making an analysis of all the skills involved and teaching these consciously. If transfer of these skills is to be gained for all other reading materials, then the child must be asked to practise each skill where it is appropriate outside the limits of the laboratory.

The major values of the laboratories would seem to be:

1   The comprehensive range of materials.
2   Emphasis upon the individual working at his correct level and his own pace.
3   The inbuilt range of materials.
4   The careful analysis of reading skills and grading of vocabulary, language structures and concepts.
5   The use of card material as a break from books.
6   The laboratories overlap in standard and therefore the very slow child can be given endless material at any one level.
7   They provide excellent material for remedial work with

children who have no specific disabilities but need coaching to reach their optimum level of development.

8   They leave the teacher more time to give individual help.

9   The stress placed upon evaluation in the reading process.

The disadvantages and weaknesses are:

1   Such material tends to give teachers the erroneous impression that their help is not necessary.

2   The material is heavily biased towards the American situation and though this is enjoyed by British children at first it has been found that they tire of it a little after a while. This is overcome to some extent in the new International Laboratory (IIA).

3   The Listening Skills have to be presented to the whole class and thus the individuality of the approach is lost here.

4   The record books are too elaborate.

5   Laboratory 1 (Word Games) is lacking in imagination and the material is difficult to adapt to one's own purposes. The discrimination of voiced and unvoiced sounds is introduced too early.

6   The Rate Builders often tend to underestimate the stage reached and therefore do not always present sufficient challenge.

7   The phonic work in the word-study section of the Power Builders is unnecessarily repetitious.

Using the laboratories for smaller amounts of time each week over the full course of the year is more time consuming and seems if anything slightly less effective in the end than the booster approach, except in the case of the slow-learning child.

The material as a whole would seem to have considerable value. The ideas behind it are excellent and it can serve the function of presenting the teacher with a ready-made structure for reading growth. This is particularly helpful when discovery approaches to learning are in operation for it teaches the child ways of reducing the time taken to locate and extract information. Indeed, outside the realm of reading laboratories, there is very little structured material for gaining the development of the higher order reading skills and most people would agree that this area of growth needs more attention than it has been given in the past.

Science Research Associates have recently introduced their International Reading Laboratory which covers the same level as the existing laboratory IIA (for children aged $7\frac{1}{2}$ to 12 years). Much of the material is new and a good amount of it has been compiled by British authors. This new laboratory should therefore overcome one of the major criticisms of British teachers that the reading material of the existing laboratories is far too much allied to American society.

Laboratories IIB and IIC have also been modified and the format of the cards and workbooks changed. Teachers who have worried about the limitations of writing only letters or single words to represent choice of answers will welcome the addition of open-ended questions which will allow more freedom and originality.

Reading Workshop (Ward Lock Educational)

This represents the first attempt by a British publisher to produce material which enters into the reading laboratory classification. As it became available as recently as June 1969 it has not been possible to carry out exhaustive tests in schools and thus the comments below must be regarded as tentative.

The Workshop has two major sections namely Work Cards and matched Speed Cards. These are graded into ten sections distinguished by colour, each section containing ten cards. The Workshop has been arranged so that each colour section represents a six-month growth in reading ability. The possession of a reading age of eight years is regarded as a minimum standard for working with the material but a number of experienced teachers have suggested that a child will need a reading age of $8\frac{1}{2}$ years at least if he is to gain reasonable success with the first colour section of the laboratory. The child records his answers in a workbook of quite simple lay-out (which fortunately is not copyright since the publishers would prefer teachers to produce their own) then marks his own work from answer cards supplied. Marking presents no problem as the child only has to check single words or letters chosen from a list of possible answers. A useful practical point is the order of the pages—the child makes a graphical representation of his progress in the centre of the workbook and when the workbook is completed the middle pages can be removed and kept for future reference whilst the answer sheets themselves can be discarded. A test card is supplied which the child can complete so as to ensure that he commences work within the Workshop at the most advantageous point.

The workcards contain a picture followed by a story or extract which the child reads before proceeding to answer comprehension and work-study questions and to work through games and exercises which have value in gaining spelling and phonic growth. The literature has a very wide range and contains imaginative stories and subject-based material.

First trials suggest that both literature and questions are greatly enjoyed by the children. The recent demand for stressing the growth of the child's ability to interpret and evaluate what is read is not reflected in the comprehension questions which are mainly at the literal level.

The Speed Cards are all to be completed in three minutes; this includes reading a short passage and answering questions on it. These would seem to be well matched to the work cards and achieve the object of reading with understanding at speed in a reasonably natural manner.

The Teacher's Handbook is a rather slim volume and though it contains helpful suggestions for organisation and administration of the work, it does not state objectives or give guidance with regard to skill growth and the help one might give children to make their approach to the reading of the cards more economical and efficient.

The manner of working suggested is that the Workshop be used for one term in three to boost attainment. During the term's usage the child would work within the laboratory every day on the basis of a three day cycle

Day	1	2	3
Task	1 Workcard	1 Workcard	2 Speed Cards

Thus each child would spend approximately 2½ hours per week on the work throughout the term. It is estimated that in a normal term the child would cover 40 Workcards and 40 Speed Cards— i.e. four colour sections. As each colour section is said to represent six months' growth in reading age we wondered if an expectation of two years reading growth is altogether realistic.

There are two major differences here in the manner of working from that of SRA Reading Laboratories. Firstly the child works through *all* ten cards within each colour section whereas in SRA a criterion of success is set at say 90 per cent correct answers and when this is achieved on three or four cards the child moves to the next section regardless of the number of cards completed. Thus in the SRA version the child has the opportunity to select the card which at first sight appeals to him. In the Workshop the child must work through every card regardless of its inherent attraction for him. Again the suggestion is made that one Workcard will be completed in a session. Average time for completion of this assignment is approximately thirty-five minutes but there are very great variations and we think the bright child could well be allowed to complete more than one card. It would in fact be interesting to experiment with the use of the Workshop under a variety of regimes.

It is felt that the *Reading Workshop* scores on its reading content but lacks a clear view of the development of reading skills. Weight has obviously been placed on the selection and writing of the literature. The questions seem to have been added afterwards. In the SRA Reading Laboratories, though the content of the questions is related to the literature, the type and structure of the questioning has been pre-determined by an analysis of the growth of reading skills. Thus the *Reading Workshop* reveals itself as having much more in common with graded reading schemes and traditional English comprehension books than does the SRA series. Which bias is the more successful in gaining good development and wider usage of reading must be left for research to ascertain.

Chapter 5 Hardware for Reading

Of all the electronic aids available to the reading teacher the tape recorder is among the cheapest and most versatile. Most schools and remedial teachers now have one such instrument and it is foreseen that the numbers in use in reading teaching will grow considerably over the years. Models can now be obtained at a reasonable price and cassette models with a switch which converts them to tape players only, means that there is little chance of children damaging the tapes in use. They can be used to provide individual work for one child, or by using a multiple outlet box and earphones up to six children can use one machine at the same time. The use of earphones is recommended for this enables such work to go on without disturbing, or being disturbed by, the noise of other activities within the classroom.

In recent years a number of taped schemes for various facets of reading work have been commercially produced. However perhaps the greatest advantage of the tape recorder is the ease with which a teacher can provide special material suited to the specific needs of her class or individuals within it. The teacher can use a tape recorder to overcome the problem of time—always the enemy of the teacher who is conscious of the necessity of giving individual attention to children within her class.

The purposes for which a tape-recorder can be used are almost endless. Auditory discrimination activities, phonic work, language development, speech training, comprehension exercises, listening skills, the introduction of new words, guided workbook exercises or simply reading a book together with the teacher are all possibilities, and no doubt there are many more.

Commercially produced taped schemes are likely to have some of the weaknesses of those aids using records in that the activities may not be exactly suited to your children or your teaching approach. One of the difficult areas is often dialect but here the offending sections can be re-recorded by the teacher. They do have the advantage of saving the teacher time and effort in the production not only of the tapes but often of accompanying books, workbooks or other activities. One assumes that they will have been tested out with children so that the final form is based on practical experience with the material. The individual teacher can only do this with personal tapes by experimentation over a period of time. A large number of the taped schemes available for purchase are specifically designed for phonic work and some of these are described in Chapter 3. Brief mention is made here of other types of work.

Pre-reading Tapes—Remedial Supply Company

This short scheme consists of six small tapes and accompanying readers and workbooks. Three other tapes and workbooks are supplied which, if used to precede this scheme, allow the child to become familiar with colours, common objects and their names. The aim of the series is to extend this knowledge to a recognition of the words in print. The vocabulary load is small but well selected and contains a number of the most used words of the English language, a few nouns which will be within every child's experience (with the possible exception of 'broom') and the more common colour names. Considerable security is given to the children in that the manner of presentation of the books and the plan of the workbooks is constant throughout the series. The titles are *Snowman, My House, Mother Goes Shopping, In the Street, The Girl* and *The Christmas Tree*. In each case the books commence with a full colour picture, then each object is introduced in turn by showing the line drawing but colouring only the object to which the text refers. The tape directs the child's work within the workbook which consists of colouring the picture step by step and writing in words over dots which ensure a worthwhile attempt. Having first completed the workbook, the child should not have any vocabulary difficulties in working through the reader.

Considerable success has been achieved with older children who had so far failed to read by making a fresh start with this material. The novelty of the tape recorder plus the security of the system appear to give the child a sense of success very quickly. Noting this we felt the scheme might profitably be used with new entrants to the infant school. We realised however that the manner of working was rather sophisticated so we re-worked both tapes and worksheets. (The Remedial Supply Company has no objection to teachers changing their materials to fit specific needs). The new tapes involved the child working first with the reader rather than the workbook. Here an attempt was made to help the child relate the picture to the text, use context, and point out specific things such as letter shapes and sounds. As the child turned to each new page the picture and text were discussed. The child then followed the text as it was read on the tape and finally read it together with the tape. The new worksheets involved colouring and simple missing-word exercises but were completed after the work with the tape so that no complications arose from switching the player on and off. These materials have now been tried in normal class environments with children aged four and five and appear to lead to speedy and effective progress within any of the popular infant reading schemes. The advantages of such early success in reading progress and attitudes towards reading is immense.

Hearing Tapes—Remedial Supply Company

Two seven-inch tapes used in conjunction with special sheets for recording responses. These have proved valuable in diagnostic work with regard to hearing, auditory discrimination and phonic work and also as material to aid the development of auditory abilities. The range of activities and types of sound particularly those drawn from real experiences in the outside world are attractive to the children. They also lead well into the Phonic Tapes produced by this publisher which are described in Chapter 3, page 43.

AUDIO-VISUAL AIDS

The Talking Page

This machine is a general audio-visual aid and is not specific to the reading situation. To date there are two stages of reading material available for use with the machine but there are also materials for use in music, mathematics and English for immigrant children. It is therefore necessary to look at the machine and the reading programmes designed for use on it separately, for the machine itself could be purchased by a school for its subject versatility which enables it to be used almost incessantly throughout a day.

In shape and size the machine is like a reading desk and consists of a record player controlled by a lever at the left-hand side. The child places the record in the machine through a slot so that there is no damage from manual operation of a playing arm and once inside the machine it cannot be touched. The child places the companion book on the top of the desk ensuring that it fits over two studs positioned at the left-hand side. Along the left hand side of the page are a number of markers which are related to a particular portion of the text. The child moves the lever until it is opposite the first marker when the record will play that section of the text and then switch off automatically. At this stage the child can push the lever up again and hear the same text or instructions repeated, or, if he feels confident, move on to the next marker and section of work. The major benefit of this machine is the possibility of immediate random access. This is not possible with complete accuracy on a record player and is very difficult on a tape recorder. Thus here the child is able to move anywhere within his book and immediately hear the odd sentence or two which he wishes, simply by pushing the lever to the correct position. Sophistication of this nature also brings a draw-back, of course, for it is impossible for the teacher to use the machine unless the commercially produced material is employed. Unlike the tape recorder, the teacher cannot therefore make up work herself to cater for needs of certain individuals within her class. Children certainly learn to use the machine very quickly and enjoy the mastery they have over it as well as the novelty of it. As such, therefore, it can be a strong motivating influence for a child whose sense of failure or general emotional instability has made it more or less impossible for him to respond to traditional material or even to the sympathetic persuasion of a teacher.

Software

First Stage Reading has been compiled by Diack and consists of 20 records and companion books and the approach is through the phonic-word method introduced by Daniels and Diack in 1956. The scheme commences with picture/sound relationships and rhyming activities at a level appropriate to the child with little or no reading skill. By the end of the twenty books the child should achieve a reading vocabulary in excess of 500 words and have gained the skills to decode many other words which are phonetically regular.

Much of the early part of the scheme concentrates upon the development of the sub-skills of reading and the teacher will no doubt feel that at a first glance there seem to be a lot of books for the ground covered. In use however with young children and non-readers aged seven it seems necessary to undertake a fair amount of supplementary work to ensure success. Of course, one would not want a young child to undertake all his reading with the help of a machine. Silent reading from other books and reading to the teacher are essential activities both for reading and personality growth.

Second Stage Reading has been prepared by Gardner and aims at structured growth in reading for those children who have attained a reading standard of at least seven years. The aims of this programme have much in common with the modern reading laboratories and workshops but the materials are somewhat different in concept. Gardner starts from interesting story material and endeavours to build in reading strategies appropriate to this stage of development. Work in comprehension, word-recognition and work-study is set but the child is always given the impression that the events of the story are of major importance.

Normal children seem to respond well to this programme, but it has been noted that some slow-learners become rather lost when constantly turning back to find the answer to a question. It would seem therefore that such children require further work of a similar type in order to progress. The major objection to the scheme is one of expense for the machine itself is too costly for most primary schools and the children's books are consumable. It is approximately five times as costly as a tape recorder and for this extra expense provides only more durable records and the advantage of random access.

The Touch Tutor

This audio-visual machine is so designed as to be easily operated by very young or sub-normal children and the material so far provided for it is concerned with pre-reading skills.

The machine is based on operant training principles. The child has to decide which of the three response panels is displaying material which correctly relates to that shown in the large stimulus panel. Having made his decision the child simply touches the panel he selects. If he is correct the machine supplies the name of the object but if incorrect makes no sound response. In either case the machine moves on automatically to the next slide which remains displayed until the child makes a further response.

Each programme consists of 100 slides which are in a rotary container and works on an internal projection system. The verbal equivalent is synchronised with each slide and is recorded on endless-loop tape. Thus the programme can be commenced at any point within the 100 frames and the whole programme will continue to circulate as many times as is necessary for the child to obtain mastery. A response-counter is incorporated and can be set so that a particular criterion rate, say 90 per cent correct responses, will be indicated by a flashing light in the control panel of the machine. Responses are recorded by photo-electric cells which also control the movement of the frames.

The machine is as yet in its experimental stage but the model we used gave a certain amount of trouble owing to incorrect sensitivity balance in the photo electric cells and the tendency of tapes to slip. One trusts that when production models are available these difficulties will have been ironed out but nevertheless the teacher will need to have some technical ability.

Five experimental programmes are at present available and these pass from the matching of colours, shapes and pictures to the matching of words to pictures. Considerable motivation and success has been reported following their usage with severely subnormal children. We used the machine in an infants class for a short period with interesting results. Its arrival occasioned immense interest and everyone wanted to sit round the new 'tele'. One takes it that the machine would eventually be accepted as a matter of routine but many intelligent children with good reading attainment were happy to spend long periods watching other children working with the machine. There can be little doubt that it has a quite magnetic attraction for children.

Two groups of children used the machine, some non-readers of below average ability and a group of normal children who had really passed through the stages covered by the programmes available. The non-readers were rather slow in their reactions and needed to have the same programme run through a number of times before mastery was achieved yet they did not appear to tire of using the machine and concentrated for rather longer than they did on normal classroom activities. The eight children in this group received sufficient help and motivation to follow the work by moving immediately to a reading scheme with some success.

The second group are not perhaps so important but produced some interesting results. One fluent reader was so quick to touch the response panel that he was rarely accurate. He became quite distressed that he wasn't getting the voice but despite advice he didn't seem to be able to exercise patience. This instance is quoted mainly as an indication of the necessity for the teacher to keep an eye on what the children are doing. Though the machine does provide, as it were, an extra person giving individual attention there are times when the total situation can only be evaluated by observation and this would not be self evident from an examination of the response counter level. In a busy classroom the changing of programmes takes rather a lot of time. However, as the machine is rather expensive it is more likely to find its way into reading clinics than classrooms and here, with a number of children requiring training in the perceptual and early reading skills, it could be a boon. It is effective in performance and highly stimulating for the children.

The Language Master

This is a simple machine consisting of a two-track tape recorder which plays tape bonded to stiff card. Thus a picture, word or letter can be presented visually to a child as he hears the appropriate sound. The child runs the card through the machine and thus the pictures and words move, not the eyes. When he feels he has mastered the content he presses the student switch, holds down the recording lever and records his response. The teacher divides any work up into fairly small units and when the child has finished a unit the teacher can check the work in a few seconds by passing the cards through the machine. Quite an extensive scheme of phonic work has been provided for use on the machine by Clift. This material is traditional in its construction and seems to have a number of inconsistencies, but a number of remedial teachers report it is effective in action.

The chief virtue of the machine lies in the fact that the teacher can quickly make up sets of individual work on the blank cards which can be obtained at a reasonable price. Thus phonic work, the introduction of new words, sentence-completion exercises and work in visual and auditory discrimination can be made for the needs of individual children. Various methods have been tried in an endeavour to use the cards for different purposes without damaging them. The best appears to be the attachment of small plastic pockets so that the visual materials can be made on a separate piece of card and simply slotted into the card bearing the tape. This means not only that the taped card can be used for other needs but also that the new material can also be stored for use on a future occasion. As it only takes a few seconds to record the text on the tape this seems a most economic and worthwhile means of preparing material. It is also possible by using plastic pockets to scheme work where a child fits a piece into a picture, a letter into a word, or word into a sentence. The machine is not much more expensive than a tape-recorder and would seem a most helpful aid in that it provides more personal work for the individual child.

It seems most successful with young children; top juniors and secondary children seem to tire of using it rather more quickly. It can of course only be used for fairly simple material as there must not be more print on the card than can be easily read in the time it takes for the card to pass through the machine. We are not aware of any evidence on the matter but wonder whether the fact that the card moves rather than the eyes could have an adverse effect on the development of good directional habits in reading. However no child should use the machine for long periods of time and if he is doing most of his reading from normal materials this should not become a problem.

The Talking Typewriter

This is the most expensive audio-visual machine available for teaching reading and is far out of the financial reach of schools. However, reading clinics in large towns could possibly make an economic proposition of it by ensuring that it was constantly used by children throughout the day and by illiterate adults in the evenings.

The machine consists of a typewriter and an internal projection slide viewer both of which arc linked to a small computer. Two major ways of working are available. The child can simply sit at the typewriter and each time he presses a key the machine will respond in sound as well as typing the letter. In this way the child learns to associate sound and symbol simply by playing at the keyboard. The machine can also be programmed so that the child works through a specific set of material. If the child does not make the correct response at any stage the programme will go over this stage again and again until the child does master it. Normally the child sits in a small booth on his own to operate the machine and therefore those children who have an emotional blockage towards teachers of reading and normal reading equipment should derive the greatest benefit.

Listen, Look, Learn Programme

This American programme will probably be available in Britain in the near future. It represents the widest use of technological equipment in a reading approach designed for general classroom use. As such therefore it could well be the herald of things to come. The basis of the programme is the division of the sub-skills needed for reading into small sequential units. Each unit or cycle concludes with a diagnostic test which should ensure that the teacher is able to guide the child to the level and activities most beneficial to his reading growth, ensuring that any sense of failure is not allowed to persist for any period of time. It is a multilevel system which allows each child to work at his own individual pace and multimodal in that provision is made for differences in learning style and competency.

Part One of the programme covers the development of the discrimination skills at the pre-reading level. Part Two concentrates on the introduction of words and endeavours to build a background of experience. Part Three is concerned with the extension of vocabulary, word study and comprehension. The material throughout is based on a mixture of whole-word and phonic approaches and therefore may be considered a mixed-methods approach. The readiness stage makes use of filmstrips to encourage the growth of visual discrimination and memory, to accompany stories and to note sounds within words. Workbooks accompany these strips giving work in spatial relationships, letter recognition and writing. Worksheets introduce puzzle approaches to the association of pictures, letters and sounds and picture sequence cards are used to extend ability to interpret pictures, follow a story sequence and tell stories orally. Synchronised filmstrips and records are aimed at the extension of the attention span, the following and interpretation of oral instructions and the study of words in specific contexts. The main section of the programme is divided into 40 cycles designed to introduce 779 sight words. This number is increased to approximately 1 200 words when the *Carousel* books for independent reading are also used and the words which the child uses for phonic practice are added.

As can be seen, the programme makes extensive use of 'hardware' as well as cards, books, worksheets and apparatus. The *Aud-X* synchronises a filmstrip with a record. As the record plays the filmstrip is controlled by a bleep outside normal hearing range. This machine is used in two ways. Firstly it introduces new sight words in sound and print simultaneously. Secondly the same procedure is used for presenting on the screen certain words which are to be learned from a story. Each time these words occur in the story they are flashed on to the screen automatically.

The *Tach-X* is a filmstrip projector with a timing device with speeds from 1/10 to 1/100 of a second. Here a word is presented, it then goes out of focus whilst the child records what he has seen in his workbook and then the word reappears in focus so that the response can be checked. This device is used to speed up recognition of words previously introduced by the *Aud-X*. The *Controlled Reader* is again basically a filmstrip projector where sections of text are illuminated at a pre-ordained rate. Use of this instrument encourages speed in reading, reading by phrase rather than word-by-word and discourages regressive eye movements. Each strip used is followed by comprehension questions ensuring that speed in silent reading does not outstrip the ability to extract ideas from the text.

The child is expected to obtain good habits of reading attack and a fair amount of vocabulary and independence in reading through the use of this hardware. During the earlier parts of the programme he will practise his skills and test his vocabulary by working through reading sheets and later by reading the *Carousel Books* and answering questions upon them which demand the ability to interpret the material as well as have a literal understanding of it. If the child has really grasped the skills and vocabulary introduced by the various machines he should be able to read the sheets and books without difficulty.

The advantages offered to child and teacher by this scheme are the careful analysis of steps in the growth of reading skill, the individualised approach with its regular checks, the motivation of an interesting range of materials and equipment and the way in which the teacher can give personal attention to problems and needs.

We think, however, that there are several disadvantages, the major one arising from the careful structuring of the material. The child can indeed work at his own pace but the manner and matter of his learning is fixed at any given stage. One of the results of research has been to point to the suggestion that children have differing styles in their approach to learning and it may be that in insisting on the development of certain skills at certain times growth may be retarded rather than encouraged. The 'hardware', though it has a place and can certainly produce results, is limiting by its very sophistication, for the teacher cannot produce records or filmstrips to use on these machines. If the teacher rigidly adheres to the materials it is difficult to link work in the skill areas to the language arts in general or to provide special individual work for any child.

It could be then that the mechanical structured approach depends on a secondary motivational factor of machine novelty rather than the more important one of a feeling of vitality in and necessity for the development of reading as a communication skill. It seems a pity also that when so much research and finance was given to the development of this programme the vocabulary was selected by analysing words used in the more popular traditional reading schemes. Most of these in turn were based on the Dolch word list which is somewhat out of date. Even a small study of present conversational speech among children would surely have given considerable benefits in this direction.

To fit a classroom up with such a range of equipment and materials is an expense far in excess of normal expenditure on reading equipment and one must ask therefore whether such expense is justified by increased effectiveness of reading instruction. To date we have no firm basis for a decision, for the material has not been the subject of research in this country.

However, our feeling is that unless hardware permits the teacher to design programmes suited to her own children's needs and allows a greater involvement with real rather than second hand experience, the tendency will be to increase the child's mechanical efficiency, but not his interest in reading as a pursuit, which is equally vital.

Chapter 6   Reflections and Recommendations

CHILD, TEACHER, METHOD AND MATERIALS

Analysing the results of the *First Grade Reading Survey* in America Professor Durrell (1968) commented that four-fifths of the variance in reading success was contributed by teacher differences and one-fifth by methodological differences. Anyone who underestimates the importance of teacher expertise, enthusiasm and level of expectancy has clearly failed to observe the classroom situation with any insight. However in any teaching/learning situation we have the child, teacher, method and materials. For study purposes we can think of these as separate entities but in practice they are closely interwoven.

The child brings with him his past development, his environment, his strengths and weaknesses, his interests and all these are reacted to by the teacher who in turn has his or her individual traits to which the child will react. Ravenette (1969) asks 'Does the child like the teacher?' and certainly it would be a rash teacher who claimed they had an equally good effect on all children. The child's interests and abilities will probably mean that he will be happier and more successful when using one set of materials and being taught through one particular approach or set of approaches and because children's abilities and interests are constantly changing it may be found that over a period of time these have to be altered to achieve maximum success. The teacher too will gain confidence and enthusiasm from the approach or approaches and materials which she is asked to use if these fit in well with her own ideals concerning the teaching of reading.

Materials therefore have a part to play in both teacher enthusiasm and expertise and the extent of progress made by the child. All too often research has concentrated upon trying to prove one method or one set of materials superior to all others and what we need now is more information about the suitability of methods and materials to children with specific abilities and disabilities and to traits within teachers. The teacher, of course, in the position of leader, must become familiar and indeed expert with more than one approach and have a variety of materials available.

Whatever the approach, method or materials in use, however, the most important factor which we can go a long way to control is the teacher's knowledge of the developmental stages of reading growth and how children can best be helped to take each step. We must recommend therefore that teachers become as familiar as possible with what knowledge has accured in this field from experience and research. Parker (1963) has suggested that education consists of two processes—'skill-getting' and 'skill-using'. 'Skill-getting' involves acquiring skills, strategies and knowledge whilst 'skill-using' is the use of these items in realistic situations. Though one would never make this sharp division in the work undertaken with children, a salutary exercise for the teacher is the making of an outline plan for their work which will isolate these areas and ensure that children are not expected to use skills of which they have no knowledge, or to learn strategies for which they have no immediate need.

Teachers would find it useful to prepare a chart in three columns. Across the columns each row would represent work of equivalent level for the average child though it will readily be seen that for individual children there will be the necessity to move various activities up or down in the columns depending on their strengths and weaknesses. Column one would contain a number of sub-divisions into further columns, each sub-division representing a skill, or strategy; for example visual discrimination, phonics, comprehension. Each of these columns would then have the detailed steps of development involved in that particular area and each step would be related by virtue of the rows to the stages in the other skills which would normally be developing at the same time.

Columns two and three would set out work for the use of these skills but, as has already been stressed, the learning and use of skills will often, and indeed should, overlap in practice. Column two would relate all other areas of the curriculum to reading. In the early stages work in art and music gives great scope for the development of visual and auditory discrimination. In discussion and later writing the child will bring his personal vocabulary and sentence structures and these should be noted and used in the development of vocabulary, word recognition and sentence patterns; work which would be carried on under the heading of Column one. This all adds vitality and realism to what could become a string of unconnected and useless bits of knowledge. In Column two also would come discovery and project work and the use of reference books. The teacher may well find it essential to plan experiences that will bring the necessity for certain skills to the notice of the children, to yield especially rich vocabulary or to extend the ability to use more complex language structures.

Column three would be a grading of all the books to fit in with the stages of development and type of work undertaken under columns one and two. The books would probably be graded in fairly broad bands and graded for total readability rather than simply graded for vocabulary growth. This is less limiting than the use of a single reading scheme but involves a disadvantage, namely, the lack of security which a reading scheme gives the child by virtue of building from a small limited vocabulary. In order to overcome this it is essential, in the early stages of reading, to ensure that the books at any stage are a little behind the skills and vocabulary development achieved under Column one. When a child learns to read from a reading scheme most of his reading is asking him to learn new words and comprehend new sentence patterns. This almost permanent state of challenge to increase knowledge of vocabulary deflects the child from the real purposes of reading, namely to find information or enjoy a story. If instruction is divorced largely from the book any difficulty in mastering a new step will not under this three-part system be automatically transferred to reading in general.

Having set up some sort of structure the teacher must beware that it does not become his/her master. It should form a framework within which to operate and should prevent Johnny being given the first thing that comes to hand when he completes his previous piece of work amidst the trials of a Monday morning. It should ensure that each step taken is related to and draws upon what has gone before and does not forbid development in any area at any later stage. For example the child who gets used to struggling from one word to the next in a graded reader as he comes each day to read aloud for the teacher is unlikely to be able to vary his reading speed according to the type of material and his purpose in reading it in the future. If however opportunity is regularly given for silent reading, sometimes of books which can be read with ease, this facility will develop to some extent quite naturally. In recent years there has been a decline in the attractiveness of story material to children. In a plan such as that outlined above it would be possible to incorporate far more practical and factual reading material and to capitalise upon the wider usage of interest and reference books which is a feature of the modern classroom.

A master chart of the skills involved in reading can be drawn up by the individual teacher with the help of the plans suggested by Della-Piana (1968) among others. It will then be necessary to convert this to a working model which reflects the preferred approach of the teacher and the needs of the children. The following example represents a unit of work which was undertaken with a group of children from a school in an educational priority area.

The children aged nine years had a reading attainment equivalent to that of the average seven-year-old.

All were somewhat retarded in language development and level of auditory discrimination. An approach based predominantly on language experience was employed and specific activities were included which were related to the reading material available. Attention was also given to the remediation of their linguistic and auditory difficulties. The individual work initiated by the children themselves cannot be represented here. Only that work pre-planned by the teacher is shown.

Further reading
MOYLE, D. (1970b) 'Planning Strategy for Reading.' *Special Education.* 59(2), 10–13.
SOUTHGATE, V. (1968) 'Formulae for beginning tuition.' *Educational Research.* 2, 23–30.

READING IN THE INFANTS SCHOOL

In the final analysis the teacher is in the best position to say if John needs a phonic approach, Sue a whole-word approach or Mary likes stories but David enjoys factual books. This individual knowledge can only accrue in that specific classroom. Certain children seem to respond to one approach rather than another. Thus great benefits can be obtained in terms of success if a careful diagnosis is undertaken before embarking on a programme of work (Strang 1970). When this is done a child can be given a feeling of success very quickly for teaching will be starting from the area of his strengths. Mills (1954) produced a structured series of lessons and tests designed to help teachers to assess which approach would be the more successful with any given child. This seems a somewhat artificial method but if trouble is taken a teacher can gain enough information to know what particular approach to use.

The majority of infant schools make extensive use of reading schemes and, though many schools have a variety of schemes, surveys (Goodacre 1967) show that in more than half of our schools one scheme forms the central part of instruction for all children though other books and apparatus may be used from time to time to supplement or extend the range of the central scheme. It is hoped that in the future capitation allowances will enable schools to have a wider range of reading materials than is usual at present and also that publishers will supply materials which provide an alternative approach to that of the reading scheme.

Remedial Supply Company's Hearing Tapes

Week	Discussion Topics	Listening Skills	Comprehension Skills	Written Work	Revision of Key Words	Special or New Words in Reader	Word Recognition Activities
1	*Keeping promises Remembering.* The story from the child's reader is used. Here a girl becomes so involved in a game she almost forgets the errand on which she had been sent.	Sequence of events. Re-telling the story.	Sequence of events. Arranging pictures in a story sequence.	Discussion of pictures from story in the Reader. Making sentences about games using the Wordmaster Major material.	*but jump then* Reading a number of sentences where the words occur in different positions.	*already forgotten leader hard think landed could caught strong* Missing word exercises.	*f m b t* as initial letters. Using first letter plus context to discover unknown words Revision using Touch cards from Stott's Programmed Reading Kit.
2	*Wishes.* The folk tale 'The Three Wishes' is told. Discussion of 'Things I wish for'.	Sequence of events. Re-arranging sentences from a story, to put them in a sensible order.	Questions on story in the Reader of the type: 'What happened next?'	Writing sentence captions for the story in the Reader. Adding a phrase to complete a sentence.	*had big little* Underlining the words in a workbook. Recognition on flash cards.	*overshoes shiny buckles time first easy help* Re-arranging jumbled sentences.	*f m b t* in medial and final positions. Rhyming games.
3	Dramatisation 'Calling the doctor'.	Carrying out instructions given orally in correct order. Topic 'Looking after someone who is sick'.	Short simple passages which the children grade as fact or fiction.	Adding an ending to an incomplete story.	*all for look* Using these words in sentences composed from Wordmaster Major materials.	*sick doctor nurse well better maybe something think* Statements to which child makes response 'True' or 'False'.	The word ending *ed*. Synthesis of regular words. Consolidation work *Sound Sense* Bk.1.

For the moment however the reading scheme holds sway and this being the situation, we must ask how best it can be used to allow the child to gain maximum growth and independence in reading. Further we must enquire how allowances can be made for the learning style and abilities of the individual child. Before these areas can be fully explored it will be necessary to examine the rationale and construction of each reading scheme employed. Considerable help can be gained here from Chapters 7 and 8 of Southgate and Roberts (1970).

The majority of reading schemes are based upon a look-say approach though few schemes are entirely 'pure' in this respect. Most include the possibility of employing sentence method and many introduce phonic work at some stage. Below is a very brief description of the methods employed in what appear to be the eleven most popular reading schemes. (For details of authors and publishers see Appendix 3).

Beacon Reading Scheme—predominantly phonic. Some opportunity is available for the use of the story method.

Gay Way Reading Scheme—phonic and sentence methods.

Happy Trio Reading Scheme—mixed methods but the early books are heavily orientated towards look-say.

Happy Venture Reading Scheme—commences with a look-say approach but phonic work is included from Book 2 onwards.

Janet and John Reading Scheme—three approaches; look-say, phonic and modified phonic. All are however heavily dependent upon the look/say approach.

Ladybird Key Words Reading Scheme—A mixed approach based on look-say and sentence method in books in Series A and B with phonic work introduced in the books in Series C.

McKee Reading Scheme—mixed methods but weighted towards look/say.

Queensway Reading Scheme—mainly look/say and sentence method.

Royal Road Readers—phonic word method with selected look/say words in the early books.

Through the Rainbow Reading Scheme—mixed methods. Emphasis is upon look/say and sentence approaches. Some opportunity to incorpoate language-experience work.

Time for Reading—mixed methods. Mainly look/say and sentence method in the early books. Later phonics and writing play a considerable part. It is also possible to fit this scheme into a language–experience approach.

Having selected and analysed the reading scheme or schemes available the next step is to ensure that pre-reading work undertaken leads naturally towards the scheme. The children should be able to use the vocabulary and types of sentence structure used in the early books in a meaningful way in their speech. Some series have pre-readers or readiness books which provide material for discussion and occasionally dramatic work. Such books also aid the development of visual and aural abilities. If such texts are not available the teacher will find it necessary to seek material elsewhere, such as Tansley's *Early to Read* books (1969). Often it will be found helpful to undertake some early work with a tape recorder to develop auditory discrimination, encourage interest and stimulate confidence within the child (see page 65).

Differing approaches within schemes require different emphases at the pre-reading stage if the child is to achieve early success. A look/say approach emphasises the relation of word to picture or object whilst a phonic one requires considerable development of auditory skills and ability to make letter/sound associations.

In the plan suggested in the last section it was recommended that actual teaching be undertaken outside the reading scheme and that books be used for enjoyment and reinforcement of skills and vocabulary taught in other ways. If, however, a reading scheme is used, not only as the instrument which structures the learning, but also as the major part of material upon which teaching and learning are to take place, then success will probably be relative to the following factors:

1 The frequency with which the child reads to the teacher. Our experience suggests that short frequent sessions are better than longer sessions held less frequently.

2 The way in which the teacher broadens the method of the scheme so ensuring that a wide range of word attack strategies are learned.

3 The opportunities given for children to consolidate their learning and derive enjoyment from reading. It would seem essential that children read regularly from books which they can read fairly easily. If only books within the reading scheme are used the child will constantly be challenged by new words and unfamiliar sentence patterns and this militates against full comprehension and thus enjoyment and satisfaction within the media.

4 The opportunities given by the teacher to relate the subject matter and vocabulary of the books to other work undertaken within the classroom.

The reading scheme offers to the teacher a growth structure and to the child a certain amount of security. It can however become restrictive. In order to gain realism and encourage independence in reading at an early date the teacher must encourage other language experiences. This can be achieved by the use of books outside the scheme and by language-experience approaches.

Further reading
MOYLE, D. (1970a) *The Teaching of Reading.* London: Ward
Lock Educational.
Chapters 4, 9, 10 and 11 deal with various aspects of early reading
growth.
SOUTHGATE, V. and ROBERTS, G. R. (1970) *Reading—Which
Approach?* London: University of London Press.
Contains a detailed evaluation of some of the reading scheme
listed above.

MATERIALS FOR REMEDIAL WORK

The selection of appropriate methods and materials for the slow-
learner and the reading failure necessitates even greater insight
than for the normal child because the range is to some extent
narrowed by what has gone before and early success is essential.
We found it a great help here to make an analysis of the materials
which have helped particular children and then list both materials
and methods according to the type of difficulty or problem
experienced so that it can be referred to quickly when we are
faced with new children. It became apparent after a time that the
children fell into four main categories with regard to the general
teaching approach required, but within each of these categories
there were often many sub-divisions. A few examples within each
of the four categories are given below and these may perhaps
serve as a basis for the reader to draw up a personal plan related
to his own stock of materials. It may also serve to indicate
gaps in the materials available to the reader which need to be
filled.

Coaching

The first division covers the many children inhabiting remedial
departments, special classes, reading clinics and the lower part of
class lists who need only coaching, that is sympathetic intensive
teaching. There are two basic types who need coaching. Firstly
there are those children of not more than nine years who are non-
readers but whose abilities and senses are normal and whose
attitudes are reasonable. The emphasis here is on early success
and speedy progress. The use of the tape recorder with simple
readers and worksheets seems to be a most efficient way of giving
some success. Often such children have passed through a regime
where only one approach, usually look-say, has been used and the
elements of a linguistic or phonic method may prove helpful.
One of the sets of phonic tapes available or a programmed series

may be matched with such schemes as *Racing to Read, Griffin Readers* and *Oxford Colour Books*. Two features are important here—first, the approach and materials should differ from those which have proved unsuccessful in the past and second, such intensive help must not suddenly cease when success is being achieved. The extra help should be faded out over a period of time.

The second group of children under the coaching heading are those who have fallen behind their optimum level because of a lack of enthusiasm or an interest in more practical pursuits. Naturally, skills which are not practised do not develop to the full. This problem is more common in boys than girls and is particularly apparent in the nine to fourteen age range. Such children, as they make some progress, are often thought to be duller intellectually than they are in fact and so go unrecognised and unhelped. These children respond to the type of booster programme provided by the SRA Reading Laboratories or the Ward Lock Reading Workshop. Some find a stimulus in speed reading programmes such as *Better Reading* or the *Craig Reader*. It is worthy of mention here that work in such programmes is only fully effective when transfer of the skills and strategies learned is made to language activities in normal work. The extent of this transfer depends largely upon the teacher knowing the stage reached and ensuring that skills learned are practised. One warning should be added here, namely, that coaching approaches are suited to retarded children—those who are very much behind what we feel to be their ability level—but not to dull children. Dull children can also become retarded but when they do success can only be achieved in a more comprehensive and less intensive learning situation.

Supplementary teaching

A number of children fall behind in reading because there are gaps in their experience or in the teaching they have received which have left them without the skills necessary to make normal progress. Such children can be said to need supplementary teaching for until the gap has been filled further progress, independence and/or fluency cannot be theirs. Many children fail to make an efficient start on reading in their early years in school as a direct result of a low level of linguistic competence due to limited speech models in their home environment. To achieve reading progress here it is necessary to expand the child's vocabulary but for most children in this group it is rather more important to enable to them use language so that they can gain a wider experience of the structure of sentences in normal speech and books.

A good deal of opportunity must be given for discussion with the teacher who will supply the new language model for the child. The beginnings of reading will be largely along language-experience lines where the teacher accepts the child's language as the basis for reading material and provides the opportunity for experiences which will be rich in the areas of vocabulary where the child is weak. For very serious cases of language deprivation the *Peabody Language Development Kit* may prove helpful and in the early stages of using books the type of language in Leila Berg's *Nipper* series may be useful. It will always be necessary with such children to ensure that the language is supplied before the reader for in the early stages of reading a child cannot expand his vocabulary or his ability to extract meaning from sentences simply by using books.

A further sub-group who require supplementary teaching is composed of children who at the top end of the junior school or in the secondary school come to a standstill in reading with a reading age of 8+ to 9+ years. On examination the reason is often found to be that the child has not developed any satisfactory word attack strategy. Such a child needs motivating by success in reading and then some sort of programme must be designed to build up his lack of skill. Often the reason is a complete reliance upon 'whole' methods in early teaching and a programme along phonic or linguistic lines proves advantageous. One of the taped schemes, Stott's kit or one of the linguistic programmed schemes may prove helpful. It must be ensured however that such work is used by the child in his general reading and that the accent on mechanics does not prevent the child reading with understanding.

A further group of children stick at roughly the same level for almost opposite reasons. These children are reasonably equipped in word recognition skills but have not developed the skill of extracting meaning from the text. Thus reading for them is a mechanical skill which seems to have little purpose and does not provide any enjoyment. These children are often helped by a considerable amount of oral work, which can be combined with or lead to work with the SRA. *Listening Tapes* and a reading laboratory or workshop will often bring success.

Remedial teaching

The third major group are those who would seem to need remedial teaching. The term remedial is used here in more or less the medical sense for a 'cure' of some sort must be effected before success can be achieved. Among this group will be those with restricting factors such as speech defects and those with grave emotional problems as well as those who have failed so often that their ambition and motivation is completely sapped. Many will need the help of psychiatry, play-therapy and speech therapy before the teacher's work can usefully commence. Some of these children are at a stage when they will not respond to teachers but they may well make an attempt to read if in comparative privacy they are allowed to work with some of the reading 'hardware'. Thus the *Touch Tutor*, the *Talking Typewriter*, the *Language Master*, the *Talking Page* or simple equipment such as the Stillitron or a tape recorder have a special place here. For teachers without such equipment Moxon's (1962) machines and charts or Webster's (1965) Visual-verbal apparatus can be manufactured relatively cheaply. Others respond to a language-experience approach whilst if the child is still young i.t.a. may afford a new start. Many children of this type have responded to the various schemes employing colour as an aid to word recognition.

Compensatory teaching

The last major type of difficulty is fortunately found less frequently than any of the above and requires long term work if success is to be achieved. It covers the children with grave specific disabilities which forbid development under normal classroom practices. For these children some sort of compensatory teaching must be made available. The purest examples here are the teaching of the deaf to lip-read and the use of braille for the blind. For otherwise normal children the two areas of difficulty most frequently met are those of visual or auditory perception. Children with visual difficulties can often be helped by Jones' *From Left to Write* or *Frostig's Programme*. One of the more interesting pieces of work in this field has been an adaptation of kineasthetic approaches by Tansley (1967) who uses what he terms a 'haptic' approach. For example a child sits behind a screen and feels articles by putting his hands through holes in the screen. By the use of touch only he must describe shape, texture, etc. in words. It has been found that many children when they have obtained a linguistic concept of shape through touch can then use this concept to improve perception in the visual sphere. Similar approaches can be used in the auditory sphere and here the *Hearing Tapes* from the Remedial Supply Company are helpful.

To achieve success in teaching reading through some such

divisions as are suggested above, it is essential that teaching be preceded by careful observation and diagnosis. Then armed with a thorough knowledge of the child, his abilities, strengths and weaknesses the teacher can plan a programme. This programme will of course have early success as its central theme so that the inhibitions of past failure can quickly be overcome. In all except the last of the four categories described above it is usually possible to commence teaching in the area of a child's strengths and only give specific attention to his weaknesses when some progress is being made. Even when it seems necessary to adopt a highly specific attack on a particular area of difficulty, however, it is unwise to lose sight of the primary objective in reading, namely extracting meaning from the printed page.

Further reading
MOYLE, D. (1969) 'Materials for remedial work in the secondary school.' *Remedial Education* Vol. 4. No. 2. pp. 85–88.

Appendix 1 Research Abstracts

i.t.a.

The two major pieces of research undertaken in Britain are reported by Downing (1967) in *Evaluating the initial teaching alphabet*. The first experiment involved 82 classes in schools widely spread throughout the country and 1 746 children divided into matched experimental (i.t.a.) and control (traditional orthography) groups. On average the experimental group learned to read more quickly. When tested in t.o. after three years this group still had significantly higher scores then the t.o. in reading accuracy. This superiority was however significantly lower than that shown prior to transfer to t.o. There was a superiority in comprehension, spelling and creative writing, though these observations were made on small sub-samples.

The first experiment was criticised on the basis of its research design and the statistical techniques employed. The second experiment, discussed by Downing and Jones in *Educational Research* (1966) though not involving such large numbers of children attempted to control some variables which were not adequately controlled in the first experiment. For example in the first experiment the experimental and control groups were normally in different schools, but in the second experiment both groups had their reading instruction from the same teacher. However there is no guarantee that individual teachers may not have been more proficient with one or other of the approaches.

Thirteen schools and some 500 children took part. Results varied considerably from school to school. Overall no statistically significant advantages were observed in either group when tested in t.o. after three years although the t.o. group had a slightly superior mean score in word recognition, comprehension and spelling.

Words in Colour

Lee (1967) in *Reading: Current Research and Practice* discusses an experiment with three matched groups of children in Ayrshire who worked respectively with i.t.a., *Words in Colour* and 'traditional methods'. After one year the children using the 'traditional methods' had an average reading age of 7 years 6 months, the

Words in Colour group 6 years 4 months, and the i.t.a. group 6 years 1 month. It is assumed that all the tests were given in normal orthography and therefore the experiment would seem to have ended far too early. Three years would have been necessary for a fair trial. No details are given of teacher expertise, enthusiasm for the materials or the actual teaching methods employed.

Brimer (1967) in *New Research in Education* reports on matched groups of children who were given the task of learning one hundred words in the following mediums: i.t.a., *Words in Colour*, Johnson's diacritical marking system, coloured words and orthodox script. Elaborate precautions were taken to overcome variables in school, teacher bias and method of presentation. The idea was simply to test what help the various mediums gave to the child in the process of decoding, not to examine their possibilities for total reading. The diacritical marking system and orthodox script were significantly superior in the number of words memorised in comparison with *Words in Colour* and i.t.a.

In *A Decade of Innovations* Hinds (1968) reports on an experiment with two matched groups taken from seventy functionally illiterate adults who worked with either traditional reading approaches or *Words in Colour*. In the *Words in Colour* group 75·8 per cent made progress as against 43·2 per cent of the group taught by traditional approaches. Actual amounts of progress are not given but the observed advantages of *Words in Colour* are discussed.

Colour Story Reading

In *Colour Story Reading: A Research Report* J. K. Jones (1967) gives an account of the main experiment involving nineteen infant schools and two pilot experiments which examined the possibilities of the scheme in remedial reading clinics and E.S.N. schools. The main experiment organised by the Reading Research Unit is very similar in design to the second i.t.a. experiment and these two experiments are compared by Jones in *Educational Research* (1968).

The major difference between the two experiments appears to be in the selection of control groups. Jones used as the control group children taught by the same teachers in the same schools whereas in the i.t.a. experiment the teachers undertook the teaching in two parallel classes within the same school, using i.t.a. with one group and t.o. with the other. This difference means that the children working with colour had the advantage of the same teacher full time whereas the i.t.a. children did not and also that teacher may have gained considerable new knowledge and enthusiasm from the colour approach which may have revitalised her reading teaching generally. Results are, not surprisingly, somewhat better than those of the second i.t.a. experiment in both word recognition and spelling but there does not appear to have been any testing of comprehension. One important factor seems to be that all children seemed to benefit more or less equally from the approach whereas in the i.t.a. experiment the brighter child benefited more than the slow-learner.

Inevitably there is the problem of the Hawthorne effect with this, as with the i.t.a. experiment. One wonders, for example, what results would have emerged if the same teachers had switched to an entirely new scheme in the third year—or even if they had returned to the old scheme.

Phonic-word Method

In *Progress in Reading* (1956) Daniels and Diack report on matched groups of children in the junior school who were taught by the same teachers using 'mixed methods'—look-say and phonics with one group and the phonic-word method with the other. The children in the phonic-word group made vastly superior progress to those in the control group.

A similar experiment to the above is described by Daniels and Diack (1966) in *Progress in Reading in the Infants School*. This involved new entrants to school and showed that similar advantages were gained by the phonic-word group.

S.R.A. Reading Laboratories

Moyle (1966) in Bulletin No. 6 of the United Kingdom Reading Association reports on a controlled trial—not a controlled experiment—involving second-, third-, and fourth-year juniors in two village schools. He investigates three areas:

1 Examination of the 'booster' principle.
2 Would SRA still effect an improvement after a class had already spent the previous term in an experimental situation using other materials new to them.
3 Would the children regress in the term after the laboratory was withdrawn.

Looking at the figures the laboratory came out on the credit side in all three areas.

In *Educational Research* Pont (1966) investigates the use of the SRA laboratories in the Midlothian schools. This was a controlled experiment involving three primary schools which tested the effect of the laboratory on reading and verbal reasoning quotients during one term, and re-tested seven months after the SRA work ended. The control groups continued with normal work throughout but the use of readers etc. seems to have been discontinued in the experimental groups whilst the SRA laboratory was being used. The experimental groups made much greater gains in reading quotients than the control groups but there was no observable effect on the verbal reasoning quotient. On retest seven months after use of the laboratory ended the experimental groups had not significantly improved in reading attainment and the control groups had more or less caught up with them.

Numerous accounts of research with various laboratories have appeared in Australia, Canada and the United States. A list of these can be obtained from Dr D. H. Parker, Emlimar, Big Sur, California 93920, U.S.A.

The Talking Typewriter

In *Remedial Education* Moseley (1969) reports on the use of the *Talking Typewriter* for remedial education. Two matched groups of ten secondary school age children were given tuition for fifteen weeks. The children of one group each had a twenty-five minute session on the typewriter each week and the children of the second group had daily sessions of twenty-five minutes on the typewriter, working in pairs in their own schools. The average attainment of both groups at the end of the fifteen weeks was the same and there was no significant difference between the groups at a later follow-up stage after tuition had ceased.

Appendix 2 List of materials discussed

Beacon Reading Scheme (1923) GRASSAM, H. London: Ginn & Co. Ltd.

Breakthrough to Literacy (1970) MACKAY, D., THOMPSON, B. and SCHAUB, P. London: Longman & Co. Ltd.

Clifton Audio Visual Reading Programme (1969) BROWN and BOOKBINDER. Stevenage: Educational Supply Association.

Colour Story Reading (1966) JONES, J. K. London: Thomas Nelson & Sons Ltd.

Day of the Week Books (1964) STOTT, D. H. Glasgow: W. & R. Holmes Ltd.

Early to Read Books (1969) TANSLEY, A. E. Leeds: E. J. Arnold & Son Ltd.

English Colour Code Tapes and Worksheets (1970) MOSELEY, D. London: National Society for Mentally Handicapped Children.

From Left to Write (1968) JONES, E. Nuneaton: Autobate Learning Systems.

Frostig Programme for the Development of Visual Perception FROSTIG, M. San Francisco: Follett Publishing Company.

Fun with Phonics (1962) REIS, M. Cambridge: Cambridge Art Publishers.

Gay Way Reading Scheme (1950) BOYCE, E. R. London: Macmillan & Co. Ltd.

Greenwood Tapes (1969) See *Key Words Reading Scheme.*

Griffin Readers (1959) MCCULLAGH, S. K., Leeds: E. J. Arnold & Son Ltd.

Happy Trio Reading Scheme (1962) First published by A. Wheaton & Co. Ltd, now Pergamon Press Ltd.

Happy Venture Reading Scheme (n.e. 1971) SCHONELL, F. J. and SERGEANT, I. Edinburgh: Oliver & Boyd Ltd.

Hearing Tapes Wolverhampton: Remedial Supply Company.

Janet and John Reading Scheme (1949) O'DONNELL, M. and MUNRO, R. Welwyn: J. Nisbet & Co.

Ladybird Key Words Reading Scheme (1964) MURRAY, W. Loughborough: Wills & Hepworth Ltd.

Language Master Wembley: Bell and Howell.

Listen, Look, Learn New York: McGraw-Hill Pub. Co. Ltd.

McKee Reading Scheme (1956) MCKEE, P., HARRISON, M. L., MCGOWAN, A. and LEHR, E. London: T. Nelson & Sons Ltd.

Merrill Linguistic Readers (1966) FRIES, C. C., WILSON, R. G. and

RUDOLPH, M. K. Columbus, Ohio: Merrill. Obtainable in Britain through Prentice-Hall International.

Nipper Books (1969) BERG, L. London: Macmillan & Co. Ltd.

Our World Series (1966) EDWARDS, R. P. A. and GIBBON, V. London: Burke Books.

Oxford Colour Books (1963) CARVER, C. and STOWASSER, C. H. Oxford: Oxford University Press.

Patterns of Sound BALDWIN, G. London: Chartwell Press.

Phonic Tapes and *Pre-reading Tapes* Wolverhampton: Remedial Supply Company.

Programmed Reading (1964) BUCHANAN, C. New York: McGraw-Hill Publishing Company.

Queensway Reading Scheme (1964) BEARLEY, M. and NEILSON, L. London: Evans Brothers Ltd.

Racing to Read (1962) TANSLEY, A. E. and NICHOLLS, R. H. Leeds: E. J. Arnold & Son Ltd.

Reading by Rainbow (1967) BLEASDALE, E. and W. Bolton: Moor Platt Press.

Rescue Reading (1968) WEBSTER, J. London: Ginn & Co. Ltd.

Royal Road Readers (1954) DANIELS, J. C. and DIACK, H. London: Chatto & Windus Ltd.

Sound Sense (1960) TANSLEY, A. E. Leeds: E. J. Arnold & Son Ltd.

Stott's Programmed Reading Kit (1964) STOTT, D. H. Glasgow: W. & R. Holmes Ltd.

Talking Page and Talking Typewriter Rank/R.E.C.

Time for Reading (1967) OBRIST, C. and PIKARD, P. M. London: Ginn & Co. Ltd.

Through the Rainbow (1965) BRADBURNE, E. Huddersfield: Schofield & Sims Ltd.

Touch Tutor Newcastle: B. R. and D. Teaching Machines.

Ward Lock Reading Workshop (1969) CONOCHIE, D. A. E., MILNE, H. E., SPENCE, J. M. and WRENCH, S. H. London: Ward Lock Educational.

Wordmaster Major London: Macdonald Educational Ltd.

Words in Colour (1962) GATTEGNO, C. London: Reading Educational Explorers.

Appendix 3 Addresses of publishers and suppliers

E. J. Arnold & Son Ltd, Butterley Street, Hunslet Lane, Leeds 10.
Autobate Learning Systems, Whitestone House, Lutterworth Road, Nuneaton, Warwickshire.
B. R. and D. Teaching Machines Ltd, 11 West View, Forest Hall, Newcastle-upon-Tyne, NE12 OJL.
Bell and Howell, Alperton House, Bridgewater Road, Wembley, Middx.
Burke Publishing Co. Ltd, 14 John Street, London WC1N 2EJ.
Cambridge Art Publishers, 3 Parker Street, Cambridge.
Chartwell Press Ltd, 84–6 Chancery Lane, London WC2.
Chatto and Windus Ltd, 40 William IV Street, London WC2N 4DF.
Educational Explorers, Silver Street, Reading, Berkshire.
Educational Supply Association, Esavian Works, Stevenage, Hertfordshire.
Evans Brothers Ltd, Montague House, Russell Square, London WC1B 5BX.
Everyweek Educational Press, High Street, Rickmansworth, Hertfordshire.
Follet Publishing Company, 201 North Wells Street, Chicago, Illinois 60606, U.S.A.
Ginn & Co. Ltd, 18 Bedford Row, London WC1.
W. & R. Holmes Ltd, 3 Dunlop Street, Glasgow.
The Longman Group, 48 Grosvenor Street, London W1.
Macmillan & Co. Ltd, 4 Little Essex Street, London WC2R 3LF.
McGraw-Hill Publishing Company, Shoppenhangers Road, Maidenhead, Berkshire.
D. G. Mitchell, Esq., (Experience-Exchange Scheme) Institute of Education, 48 Old Elvet, Durham.
Moor Platt Press, Bolton.
National Society for Mentally Handicapped Children, Centre for Learning Disabilities, 86 Newman Street, London W1P 4AR.
Thomas Nelson & Sons Ltd, 36 Park Street, London WIY 4DE.
J. Nisbet & Co. Ltd, Digswell Place, Welwyn Garden City, Hertfordshire.
Oliver & Boyd Ltd, Tweedale Court, 14 High Street, Edinburgh 1.
Oxford University Press, Walton Street, Oxford.
Pergamon Press Limited, Headington Hill Hall, Oxford OX3 0BW.

Prentice-Hall International Inc., Durrants Hill Road, Hemel Hempstead, Hertfordshire.

Rank/R.E.C., 11 Belgrave Road, London SW1.

Remedial Supply Company, Dixon Street, Wolverhampton.

Schofield and Sims Ltd, 35 St John's Road, Huddersfield, Yorkshire.

Science Research Associates, Reading Road, Henley-on-Thames, Berkshire.

Stillit Books Ltd, New Bond Street, London W1.

Ward Lock Educational Co. Ltd, 116 Baker Street, London W1M 2BB.

Wills and Hepworth Ltd, Derby Square, Loughborough, Leicestershire.

Bibliography

BALDWIN, G. (1967) *Patterns in Sound*. London: Chartwell Prees.

BRIMER, A. (1967) 'An experimental evaluation of coded scripts in initial reading.' In WALL, W. D. (ed.) *New Research in Education*. Slough: National Foundation for Educational Research.

BURROUGHS, G. E. R. (1957) *A Study of the Vocabulary of Young Children*. London: Oliver & Boyd.

BURT, C. (1967) Foreword to WALL, W. D. (ed.) *i.t.a. Symposium*. Slough: National Foundation for Educational Research.

CHALL, J. S. (1967) *Learning to Read: The Great Debate*. New York: McGraw-Hill.

DANIELS, J. C. and DIACK, H. (1956) *Progress in Reading*. Nottingham: University Institute of Education.

DANIELS, J. C. and DIACK, H. (1966) *Progress in Reading in the Infant School*. Nottingham: University Institute of Education.

DIACK, H. (1960) *Reading and the Psychology of Perception*. Nottingham: P. Skinner.

DOWNING, J. A. (1967) *Evaluating the Initial Teaching Alphabet*. London: Cassell.

DOWNING, J. A., and JONES, B. (1966) 'Some Problems of Evaluating i.t.a.: a Second Experiment.' *Educ. Res.*, 8, 100–14.

DELLA-PIANA, G. M. (1968) *Reading Diagnosis and Prescription: An Introduction*. New York: Holt, Rinehart & Winston.

DURRELL, D. (1968) Chapter in VILSCEK, E. C. (ed.) *A Decade of Innovations*. Newark, Delaware: I.R.A.

EDWARDS, R. P. A., and GIBBON, V. (1964) *Words Your Children Use*. London: Burke Publishing Co.

FLESCH, R. (1955) *Why Johnny Can't Read*. New York: Harper Row.

FRIES, C. C. (1962) *Linguistics and Reading*. New York: Holt, Rinehart & Winston.

FRY, E. A. (1966) In MONEY, J. (ed.) *The Disabled Reader*. New York: Hopkins.

GATTEGNO, C. (1962) *Words in Colour: Background and Principles*. Reading: Educational Explorers.

GODDARD, N. L. (1969) *Reading in the Modern Infants' School* (2nd Edn) London: University of London Press.

GOODACRE, E. J. (1967) *Reading in Infant Classes*. Slough: National Foundation for Educational Research.

HINDS, L. R. (1968) 'Studies in the use of colour'. In VILSCEK, E. C.

(ed.) *A Decade of Innovations*. Newart, Delaware: I R A.

HODGES, R. E. and RUDORF, E. H. (1965) 'Searching linguistics for cues for the teaching of spelling.' *Elementary English*. **42**, 527–33.

JAGGER, J. H. (1929) *The Sentence Method of Teaching Reading*. London: Grant.

JONES, J. K. (1965) 'Colour as an aid to visual perception in early reading.' *Br. J. educ. Psychol*. **35** (1), 22–7.

JONES, J. K. (1967) *Colour Story Reading: A Research Report*. London: Nelson.

JONES, J. K. (1968) 'Comparing i.t.a. with Colour Story Reading.' *Educ. Res*. **10**(3), 226–34.

LEE, T. (1967) 'Writing the talking: an appraisal of Words in Colour.' In BROWN, A. L. *Reading: Current Research and Practice*. Edinburgh: Chambers.

LEFEVRE, C. (1964) *Linguistics and the teaching of reading*. New York: McGraw-Hill.

MCNALLY, J. and MURRAY, W. (1962). *Key Words to Literacy*. London: Schoolmaster Publishing Co.

MERRITT, J. E. (1967) 'The S.R.A. Laboratories.' In BROWN, A. L. (ed.) *Reading: Current Research and Practice*. Edinburgh: Chambers.

MERRITT, J. E. (1968) 'The linguistic approach to reading.' In DOWNING, J. A. and BROWN, A. L. (eds.) *Third International Reading Symposium*. London: Cassell.

MILLS, R. E. (1954) *Learning Methods test*. Fort Lauderdale Mills Centre Inc.

MORRIS, R. (1963) *Success and Failure in Learning to Read*. London: Oldbourne.

MOSELEY, D. V. (1969) 'The Talking Typewriter and Remedial Teaching in a Secondary School.' *Remedial Educ*. **4**(4), 196–202.

MOXON, C. A. V. (1962) *A Remedial Reading Method*. London: Methuen.

MOYLE, D. (1966) 'A Report on the use of the S.R.A. Reading Laboratory IIA.' Bulletin No. 6 of United Kingdom Reading Association.

MOYLE, D. (1969) Materials for remedial work in the secondary school. *Remedial Educ*. **4**(2), 85–88.

MOYLE, D. (1970a) *The Teaching of Reading*. 2nd Edn. London: Ward Lock Educational.

MOYLE, D. (1970b) 'Planning Strategy for Reading.' *Special Educ*. **59**(2), 10–13.

MURPHY, M. L. (1968). *Douglas Can't Read*. Reading: Educational Explorers.

MURRAY, W. (1969). *Teaching Reading*. Loughborough: Wills & Hepworth.

PARKER, D. H. (1963) *Schooling for Individual Excellence*. New York: Nelson.

PIAGET, J. (1956) *The Child's Conception of Space*. London: Routledge & Kegan Paul.

PONT, H. (1966) 'An investigation into the use of the S.R.A. Reading Laboratory in the Midlothian Schools.' *Educ. Res.* Vol. VIII(3), 230–36.

RAVENETTE, A. T. (1969) *Dimensions of Reading Difficulty*. Oxford: Pergamon.

ROBINSON, H. M. (ed.) (1968) 'Innovation and Change in Reading Instruction.' *N.S.S. E. Yearbook 67*. Pt. 2. Chicago: Chicago University Press.

RUDDELL, R. B. (1965) 'The effect of similarity of oral and written language patterns on reading comprehension.' *Elementary English*, **42**.

SCEATS, J. (1967) *i.t.a. and the Teaching of Literacy*. London: Bodley Head.

SCHONELL, F. J. (1949) *Psychology and the Teaching of Reading*. Edinburgh: Oliver & Boyd.

SOUTHGATE, V. (1968) 'Formulae for beginning reading tuition.' *Educational Research* Vol. II, 23–30.

SOUTHGATE, V. and ROBERTS, G. R. (1970) *Reading: Which Approach?* London: University of London Press.

STOTT, D. H. (1964) *Roads to Literacy*. Glasgow: W. & R. Holmes.

STRANG, R. (1970) *Diagnostic Teaching of Reading* 2nd Edn. New York: McGraw-Hill.

TANSLEY, A. E. (1967) *Reading and Remedial Reading*. London: Routledge & Kegan Paul.

TUDOR-HART, B. (1969) 'An Experiment in Teaching Method Using i.t.a. 1964–68.' (unpublished report) London: i.t.a. Foundation.

VILSCEK, E. C. (ed.) (1968) *A Decade of Innovations*. Newark, Delaware: I.R.A.

WARBURTON, F. W. and SOUTHGATE, V. (1969) *i.t.a. An Independent Evaluation*. London: Murray/Chambers.

WEBSTER, J. (1965) *Practical Reading*. London: Evans.

Index

Modern innovations in the teaching of reading